THE LIBERATORS OF BANGLADESH

BY THE SAME AUTHOR

The Kargil Story

THE LIBERATORS OF BANGLADESH

GLORIOUS BATTLES FROM THE 1971 INDO-PAK WAR

DEEPAK SURANA

An imprint of
Srishti Publishers & Distributors

Srishti Publishers & Distributors
A unit of AJR Publishing LLP
212A, Peacock Lane
Shahpur Jat, New Delhi – 110 049

editorial@srishtipublishers.com

First Published by Bold,
an imprint of Srishti Publishers & Distributors in 2024

10 9 8 7 6 5 4 3 2 1

This is a work of non-fiction based on the author's research about the subject and interviews with their next of kin, friends and associates. While due care has been taken by the author and publisher to verify contents at press time, any inadvertent miss that is brought to their notice shall be duly verified and updated subsequently. Actual names of people and places have been used with a view to provide first-hand information.

Maps used in the book are for representation purposes only.

Printed and bound in India

CONTENTS

FOREWORD

Quite literally, time flies! It's already fifty-three years to our magnificent victory over the enemy in the 1971 War. Time has taken its rightful course and now, in my late eighties, I stand in the twilight of my life. However, memories from those days – when I led the daring boys of *Raghupratap*[1] as their Commanding Officer, to break the enemy's back in the Jessore sector – are still fresh in my mind.

A part of me is still on the battlefields of Maslia, Burinda and Syamganj with the fifty-one battalion brave-hearts who were killed in action giving their all for the country they loved so much. Their cries of pain after being hit badly by splinters and bullets still pierce my heart. I have woken up on many a dark night, with beads of sweat lining my forehead, as the battles play out repeatedly in my dreams.

My heart still cries for men like Umesh Gupta and Meghraj, among others. They were young boys, in the prime of their youth, who did not bat an eyelid before doing outrageously brave things in the war without a thought for personal safety. Each hero who died carried a piece of me with him.

---

1 Another name given to 1st Jammu and Kashmir Rifles

Over a course of thirty-seven days in late 1971, my battalion first trained the Mukti Bahini and then fought decisive battles at Maslia and Syamganj. While the former was a defensive battle fought a few kilometres inside enemy territory, the latter was the first major offensive against Pakistan's 107 Infantry Brigade deep inside the Khulna sector. Our victory at Syamganj sealed the fate of the enemy in the Jessore-Khulna sector.

I can proudly claim that my unit, the 1st Jammu and Kashmir Rifles (1st JAK Rifles), was one of the first battalions to enter East Pakistan and one of the last to return to our side of the border after the cessation of hostilities. While I was decorated with the Maha Vir Chakra (MVC) for my leadership and gallantry, my battalion braves also received three Vir Chakras and four Sena Medals. We were also bestowed with the battle honour of 'Syamganj' and the theatre honour of 'East Pakistan'.

I strongly believe that my gallantry award belongs to each soldier of my battalion who contributed immensely to the war effort. Without their collective efforts, victory was impossible. I wear the gallantry medal on my chest on their behalf! My soft-spoken Dogra boys, hailing from the mountains of Himachal Pradesh, the plains of Jammu, and Northern Punjab, proved to be more than a match for the Pakistan army.

Somehow, over the years, the achievements of my battalion went unnoticed in the coverage of the 1971 War. Despite being declared as the best Battalion of our Army's 9th Infantry Division, I believe we did not get the due we deserved. While our success has been highly revered in the Army circles, the common citizen has no clue about the Battle of Syamganj! More publicised battles, which I do not wish to mention about, have caught the imagination of the public.

When the young and energetic Deepak contacted me three years ago, wanting to write about the actions of my unit in 1971, I could see a ray of hope. With bestselling books like, *The Shershah Of Kargil* and *The Kargil Story* to his credit, I was certain that he was the best man to tell the story of my battalion.

Talking to him on many occasions over the phone and meeting him once at my place in Delhi made me realise the deep passion and love he has for the Indian Army, despite coming from a 'non-*fauji*' family. His grip over military lingo and interest in battle tactics truly amazed me! His attention to detail, no matter how significant or insignificant the incident was, is commendable.

With the help of handwritten notes I had sent him and the numerous interactions he had with me and my officers, Deepak has been able to present a graphic and blow-by-blow account of the actions of my battalion. His touching and impactful description of the war scenes has added a whole new human touch to it. I am thankful to him for covering those acts of bravery and sacrifice which have never been out in the public domain before.

I am glad that finally there is a detailed record of my Battalion's exploits from the 1971 War. As they say, better late than never! I really hope and wish that this book strikes a chord with the readers and goes a long way in inspiring youngsters to join the Armed Forces.

— Lieutenant Colonel Surinder Kapur, MVC

February 2024, New Delhi

PREFACE

The victory at Syamganj was one of the most significant contributions made by my regiment, the JAK Rifles, during the Bangladesh Liberation War in 1971. It still remains a peerless saga of courage, sacrifice and extra-ordinary leadership against heavy odds. The grit and determination shown by all ranks of the Raghupratap Battalion in those tough times serves as a lesson for all the troops of this illustrious and highly decorated regiment.

While this battle is well-known and still spoken about in our regimental circles, it has not been covered in its entirety till now, even fifty-three years after it was fought so gallantly. Even in the large voluminous books and documentaries on the 1971, this battle, somehow, only got a fleeting mention here or there.

This, despite the fact that the battalion lost fifty-one of its brave-hearts and was decorated with a host of gallantry awards, including one Maha Vir Chakra, three Vir Chakras and four Sena Medals during the War. The battalion fought tooth and nail to achieve resounding victories on the battlefields of the Jessore-Khulna sector.

Way back in the year 1982, when I was commissioned into this prestigious regiment as a young 2nd Lieutenant, I heard about this battle for the first time during my induction at the JAK Rifles

Regimental Centre at Jabalpur. This victory and the other significant victories of the regiment over a period of two centuries, served as a big motivation for me and my boys of *Teevra Terah* (13 JAK Rifles) as we pushed back enemy intruders in the Drass and Mushkoh sub-sectors during the Kargil War in 1999.

As the former Colonel of the Regiment, it gives me immense joy and pleasure to commend Deepak for choosing to write in detail on this unsung battle fought by the heroes of my regiment. This is his third book and I wish him the very best for it. Incidentally, all his books very strongly feature and describe in detail the actions of the heroes from the JAK Rifles regiment. The richly and vividly sketched war scenes are a delight to read and the deep research is there for everyone to see.

I am also glad that Retd Lt Col Surinder Kapur, MVC – the then Commanding Officer of 1st JAK Rifles – very graciously and magnanimously contributed during the research of the book despite his old age. He is the true epitome of humility and chivalry. Deepak couldn't have asked for a better mentor and guide to write this richly detailed book.

I am sure that this book will be a very welcome addition to our rich military literature and folklore and will inspire young boys and girls even decades later. Books on military heroes are the foundations on which proud nations are built! Jai Hind!

— Lieutenant General Y.K. Joshi,
PVSM, UYSM, AVSM, VrC, SM
(Former General Officer
Commanding-in-Chief Northern Command)

AUTHOR'S NOTE

The victory over Pakistan in the 1971 War stands out as one of India's most glorious moments in her checkered history since Independence from the British in 1947. Post War, India emerged as a clear-cut leader among the sub-continental countries. It was a victory engineered by decisive political leadership and supreme military performance. Pakistan, that for many years had harboured the dream of seizing a sizeable chunk of Indian territory, was literally cut down in size.

By the end of the war, East Pakistan was reborn as a new nation called Bangladesh. A year of unrest and struggle had finally come to an end. To protect the sovereignty and safeguard the human rights of the citizens of East Pakistan, the Indian Armed Forces jumped into the fray and launched offensives to dislodge Pakistan's army from East Pakistan.

The result was the surrender of 93,000 Prisoners of War (POWs) – the highest since World War II.

The 1971 War is often dubbed as a 'fourteen-day war,' as the war officially began on 3 December 1971 and ended on 16 December 1971, with the surrender of the Pakistan army. However, there were a few battalions of the Indian Army for whom the war started in early November – almost a month before the official declaration of war.

One such battalion was the 1st JAK Rifles, also known as Raghupratap, led by the feisty Lt Col Surinder Kapur. This legendary battalion, on Pakistan's provocation, entered East Pakistan in the second week of November and beat back five enemy counter-attacks at Maslia. Two weeks later, it was again in action at Burinda to dislodge a numerically superior enemy.

It was among the first battalions to reach Jessore and report to the Brigade Headquarters that the city had fallen without a fight. The battalion's finest hour came on 15 December, when in a daylight assault, it captured the enemy stronghold at Syamganj and virtually broke down the door leading to Khulna.

A couple of days later, the valiant and astute Commander of Pakistan's 107 Infantry Brigade, Brigadier Muhammad Hayat, and many others from Pakistan army surrendered to the Commanding Officer of the unit, signalling the end of hostilities in the 1971 War. Thus, the 1st JAK Rifles, which was one of the first battalions to enter East Pakistan, was the last to get back to India – making it a 'thirty-five-day' war for them!

The unit lost fifty-one of its gallant heroes and more than a hundred were injured, some disabled for life. Lt Col Kapur was awarded the MVC for his bravery and leadership, while three VrCs and four SMs besides a host of other gallantry awards were bestowed on the braves of the unit. Following a thorough review, the unit was given the battle honour, 'Syamganj', and theatre honour, 'East Pakistan'.

Over the years, I have laid my hands on many outstanding books written about the 1971 War. The battles fought at Basantar, Longewala, Garibpur, Hilli and Dacca have become a part of our rich military folklore. These battles and the heroes who fought in them have received rightful celebration across news channels, theatre plays, movies, books, and comics; their presence evident in army cantonments and stations.

The Battles of Maslia and Syamganj, despite being equally fierce and important, however, remained in obscurity. My thirst to gather more information about the JAK Rifles regiment led me to discover the number of battle honours the regiment has been conferred with. Syamganj is one of the hard-earned battle honours the regiment received for its actions during the 1971 War.

To my surprise, I hardly found anything about this battle on various platforms. All I could gather was that Lt Col Surinder Kapur, MVC, was the CO of the unit during the war. As luck would have it, in early 2021, after months of searching, I found the retired Colonel's number on TWDI,[2] much to my joy and elation.

Two long and delightful telephonic conversations with the octogenarian triggered in me the idea of writing a book on the unsung battles fought by him and his brave unit. As we delved deeper and went back in time to piece together the events that took place fifty-one years ago, Retd Lt Col Kapur graciously promised to send me, in writing, his memories from those fateful days.

---

2 The War Decorated India, https://twdi.in/

Despite being well into his late eighties, Retd Lt Col Kapur painstakingly compiled his recollections and sent them within six months of his promise. Meeting him for the first time in January 2023 on a cold Delhi afternoon has been one of the finest moments of my life. We sat together on his lawn for over four hours, with a golden retriever for company, to relive the 1971 War.

I sat listening in rapt attention, as the dynamic Lt Col narrated every bit of what his photographic memory had in store. He roughly sketched and showed what the Jessore sector – with rivers like the Kabadak and Bhairab, and towns like Jessore and Khulna – looked like. As a writer, I couldn't have asked for more from the protagonist of this book. The icing on the cake was when Retd Lt Col Kapur, on my request, immediately agreed to collaborate on this book and fill in the gaps wherever needed.

Col Jasbir Sarai and Col Harnam Billawaria, two other heroes from the 1st JAK Rifles, were also interviewed multiple times for their accounts. The official history of the unit was also accessed, thanks to the current CO and his wonderful officers. Schematic maps and sketches added in the book were received from the battalion and so were the names of the fifty-one unit braves killed in action.

This book is my sincere attempt to bring the Battles of Maslia and Syamganj into the public consciousness. This is a saga of consistent bravery, which should not have been under the carpet for such a long time. I am sure the selfless acts of valour performed by 2nd Lieutenant Umesh Gupta and Lance Naik Meghraj, among others from the battalion, will inspire military personnel and civilians alike.

The battalion's move to the border in early 1971, its role in training the Mukti Bahini and their actions during the thirty-five days form the crux of this book. Interpersonal relationships between the officers, JCOs and *jawans* are an important part of the book.

A few dialogues between the characters have been recreated to add flow to the book. A genuine effort has been put into maintaining high levels of accuracy throughout the book. Outstanding acts of individual and collective gallantry by the battalion heroes have been richly and vividly described.

I am sanguine that, after reading this book, the readers will get a fresh perspective of the 1971 War through the lens of the 1st JAK Rifles. I am sure that this book will add freshness and colour to the already richly painted canvas of the literature of the 1971 War.

Jai Hind!

— *Deepak Surana*

9 January 2024

INTRODUCTION

In December 1970, General Yahya Khan, the military dictator and President of Pakistan, ordered the first-ever general elections in Pakistan since its independence in 1947. The result was an astounding victory for the Awami League of East Pakistan, led by the much-loved Bengali leader, Sheikh Mujibur Rahman.

This was unacceptable to his fierce rival, the kingpin of the Pakistan People's Party, Zulfikar Ali Bhutto. From the Sindh region of West Pakistan, Bhutto was vehemently against being led by a Bengali leader from East Pakistan. Gen Yahya Khan backed him and did not hand over the reins of the federal government to Sheikh Mujibur Rahman.

The suspension of the National Assembly and delay in the transfer of power triggered unrest in East Pakistan. Over the last twenty-four years, they had been victims of suppression and step-motherly treatment from the West Pakistani elite. On 7 March 1971, Mujibur Rahman addressed the people of East Pakistan from Dacca (now Dhaka) and made it clear that the eventual goal of the Awami League was total independence from the clutches of West Pakistan.

To curb the unrest and uprising, Gen Yahya Khan ordered a crackdown in East Pakistan, codenamed Operation Searchlight. The overall command of the operation was given to Major General Tikka Khan, also known as the Butcher of Baluchistan.

On 25 March 1971, troops from Pakistan army stormed Dacca University and killed numerous Bengali intellectuals and students who were protesting against the injustice being meted out by the bosses controlling West Pakistan. Around the same time, similar raids were engineered across East Pakistan.

Bengali houses were burned, their men beheaded and women raped mercilessly. Children were not spared either, as they were shot dead by the ruthless troops of Tikka Khan. Those who escaped crossed over to the Indian border states of West Bengal, Assam, Meghalaya and Tripura to seek refuge.

The atrocities continued for months, and the number of refugees coming to India rose. India's bold Prime Minister, Mrs Indira Gandhi, toured the world to gather international support, but the response she got was more than disappointing. When she expressed the increasing burden on Indian resources because of the refugee crisis caused by West Pakistan's aggression, the then President of the USA, Richard Nixon, brushed it aside as Pakistan's internal matter and refused to intervene. Barring Russia, no other major power sided with India.

Meanwhile, under the overall command of Gen Sam Manekshaw, the Indian Armed Forces prepared themselves for military intervention in East Pakistan. Gen Manekshaw, despite political pressure, was clear that he would attack the enemy at the place and time of his choosing. He factored in the terrain of East Pakistan, the preparation of his troops and the cohesion of the three services before zeroing in on a tentative date for military intervention. Able-bodied refugees, who had earlier been in the Pakistan police or army, were trained by Indian battalions and a force named Mukti Bahini (freedom fighters) was born.

By early November 1971, it became certain that using military might was the only option, in retaliation to unprovoked fire by the Pakistan army on Indian border outposts, small columns of the Mukti Bahini and the Indian Army crossed the border and captured vital ground, despite stiff Pakistani resistance. By this time, the number of refugees in India had reached ten million.

On 3 December 1971, pre-emptive strikes by Pakistan Air Force on vital Indian Air Force bases marked the start of a full-fledged war. Within fourteen days of fierce fighting, the gallant officers and men from the Indian Armed Forces, put to dust Pakistan's challenge. On 16 December 1971, 93,000 Pakistani POWs, led by Lt Gen Niazi, surrendered to the might of India at Dacca. East Pakistan became Bangladesh, Pakistan lost territory and was humiliated, and India proved its military might to the world.

This war also brought to light the brilliant cohesion between the Indian Army, the Indian Navy, and the Indian Air Force (IAF). The ground troops penetrated deep inside East Pakistan, fighting inch by inch while also defending our Western borders tenaciously; the IAF pilots brought down numerous Pakistani F-86 Sabre jets in dogfights and bombed vital enemy military bases and installations. The skill and gumption shown by the fighter pilots of the IAF was a lesson for pilots across the globe.

The Indian Navy, notoriously referred to as the 'Cinderella' service, shed this tag by playing a decisive role in the war. Under the direction of Admiral Nanda, the Indian missile boats operating in the Arabian Sea bombed and virtually destroyed the Karachi harbour, Pakistan Navy's main headquarters. Karachi harbour was burning for many days. The Indian sailors sank many ships of the Pakistan Navy, ranging from destroyers to minesweepers.

The aircraft carrier and pride of the Indian Navy, *INS Vikrant*, operated in the Bay of Bengal and pounded Pakistan's strategic assets and communication hubs at Chittagong, Cox's Bazar, and Khulna. Sea Hawks and Alize aircraft catapulting from it created havoc in East Pakistan and effectively blocked all the enemy routes for escape.

Thus, the victory in the 1971 War marked India's finest hour since her independence in 1947. It resulted from decisive political will, proactive military leadership, and most importantly, the courage and sacrifices of the men in uniform.

PRELUDE

Somewhere in Arunachal Pradesh
Early January 1971

Lt Col Surinder Kapur, the CO of the 1st JAK Rifles, is up in the hills for a route march with his boys when he receives a call from the Brigade Headquarters. It's quarter past nine in the chilly morning, an odd time to get such a call. In the Army, however, Lt Col Kapur knows that there is nothing known as an 'odd time'. Orders can come at any moment, without warning.

'Lt Col Kapur, cancel your route march immediately and report to the Brigade Headquarters. We have sent a Jeep for you. The Brigadier will brief you further,' informs a staff officer.

'I will be there. Roger.'

Making his way down the winding roads in a Military Gypsy, Lt Col Kapur ponders over the reason behind his immediate summon. Originally from the Gorkha Rifles regiment, he had taken over the command of 1st JAK Rifles near Bomdila six months ago. The operational role given to the battalion in mountainous terrain has given him a chance to familiarize himself with their ways of working and understand their psyche.

During his time with the battalion, he has observed that the junior leaders – the young lieutenants, captains, and majors – are highly charged-up men. He has also noted that the experienced JCOs and NCOs have done extremely well to inculcate the spirit of camaraderie and regimentation in the young troops of the unit. He is certain that, if given the right leadership, the battalion can do wonders.

At the Headquarters, once the pleasantries are exchanged, the Brigadier gets talking, 'Lt Col Kapur, prepare your battalion to move to Missamari immediately. Transport has already been arranged.'

Standing in crisp attention, Lt Col Kapur replies, 'Right, sir. It will be done. May I know where exactly our next posting is?'

'It's a temporary posting, Colonel. Rail coaches have been arranged. Your battalion will move to West Bengal from Missamari, Assam,' the Brigadier clarifies.

'What will be our task, sir?' asks Lt Col Kapur, wanting some information on the topic.

'I am not quite sure about it. Report to 9 Infantry Division for further orders.'

'Sure, sir. Jai Hind.'

Two days later, Lt Col Kapur and his troops find themselves at the Missamari railway station, waiting to catch the train that will take them to West Bengal. The hardy Dogra troops unwind at the platform, as the wait for the train is long. Some are writing letters back home while others huddle up together and sing their hearts out. Havildar

Sukhdev Singh, the Regimental Police platoon Havildar, is the life of the group as he enchants his comrades with his rendition of Dogri and Punjabi folk songs.

Lt Col Kapur, who is watching all of this from a distance, cannot suppress his smile. He has been very strict and upright with his men, but lets them enjoy such occasions. He knows such moments will come few and far between, considering the profession they are in. He hums along soundlessly to a few Punjabi songs he knows. After a long wait, he sees a train at a distance, chugging along the tracks and approaching the platform in all its glory.

Following a long and arduous journey, the train stops at Midnapore station. A few staff officers of 9 Infantry Division and 9 Artillery Brigade come to receive them. Within minutes, all the troops, with their large olive green and black Army trunks, assemble neatly in Company groups at the platform guided by their Company Commanders and other officers.

'Welcome, sir. This is the destination of the 1st JAK Rifles,' says a staff Major, smartly passing a salute to Lt Col Kapur.

Acknowledging the young man, Lt Col Kapur speaks with a tinge of sarcasm, 'Thank you, young man. Finally, the CO of 1st JAK Rifles knows where his boys will operate.'

'Pardon me, sir, we were ordered to keep the location a secret due to the prevailing threat of Naxals in West Bengal,' the Major reasons.

Taking a deep sigh, the Lieutenant Colonel moves on to important questions, 'Where do we report now?'

'Sir, your unit can set up their camps now. You will have to report to the Headquarters of 9 Artillery Brigade for further orders,' the Major answers.

After spending the entire night supervising the camp setup, Lt Col Kapur reports to the Headquarters of 9 Artillery Brigade. He is informed that his battalion has been deployed in Midnapore to provide internal security during the upcoming West Bengal elections. Trouble in the form of riots is expected prior to and during the elections. The battalion is also tasked to carry out regular flag marches as a show of strength and confidence to deal with any untoward activities by the mobs.

Additionally, Lt Col Kapur and the other officers carry out a thorough reconnaissance of the places where the election booths would be set up and the spots where trouble is likely to start prior and during the polling. To the credit of 1st JAK Rifles, not a single unruly incident takes place in their area of responsibility, and the elections go smoothly. During the four months, seeing the discipline and tact with which his officers and men have performed their tasks, Lt Col Kapur is pleased as punch.

One typical spring afternoon, the General Officer Commanding, 9 Infantry Division, Maj Gen Dalbir Singh, accompanies the Eastern Army Commander, Lt Gen Jagjit Singh Aurora on a visit to the unit. Very pleased with what he has seen and heard about 1st JAK Rifles, Lt Gen Aurora praises the unit. He is particularly impressed by the stick orderly[3] of the CO, Rifleman Sindoor Singh, and promotes him to the rank of Lance Naik.

Soon after the elections, the battalion is sent to Siuri in Birbhum, a district bordering Bihar. The unit packs up once again and moves to tackle the growing naxalism and militancy. Here, the Charlie Company eliminates a dreaded Naxal commander, who would loot innocent people and beat them up mercilessly. It is a well-planned encounter, and the situation is brought under control.

Besides tackling the Naxal menace, the unit also sets up an outpatient camp to give free treatment to the largely poor population of Birbhum. Funds for the clinic are arranged by the battalion and through the personal contributions of officers. Capt A.L. Sharma, the Regimental Medical Officer (RMO), does exceedingly well in bringing down the impact of life-threatening diseases in the area. Maj Gen Dalbir Singh is mightily impressed with the performance and professionalism of the 1st JAK Rifles. His previous liking for the unit soon catapults to supreme confidence and faith in their abilities.

THE CALL

March 1971

One day, as Lt Col Kapur leisurely sips lemonade with his fellow officers at the battalion headquarters in Siuri, the huge olive-green telephone placed on a desk close to him rings. Hurriedly stepping forward to answer the call, Lt Col Kapur's pose stiffens as he speaks. Noting a marked change in his posture, his junior officers fathom the

---

3 A soldier assigned to undertake tasks for the highest ranking officer at a location.

call to be from the higher ups. Suddenly, the Lieutenant Colonel's entire demeanour shifts. He smiles as he keeps the receiver down.

Lt Col Kapur exudes his usual swagger as he walks back to his officers. Gathering his things with a calmness that displays years of experience, he says, 'Gentlemen, there is some good news. We have been ordered to move to the East Pakistan border in a few days. We might see action soon.'

Unable to contain their excitement, Maj Harnam Billawaria, 2nd Lt Umesh Gupta and 2nd Lt Jasbir Sarai rise from their chairs and cheer. They expected this call because of the rapidly declining situation in East Pakistan, but it has come much earlier than they anticipated.

Moments after the announcement is made, the mood of the entire battalion lifts. For them, the last three months have been uneventful. The battalion had been deployed to look after the internal security for the smooth conduct of elections in West Bengal, something that most soldiers dislike. The call to go to the border gives the soldiers a chance to do what they have been trained for.

As he strolls out of the Headquarters, soaking in the magnificent early summer sun, Lt Col Kapur summons the young and bold Sikh officer, 2nd Lt Jasbir, to pass urgent orders, 'Jasbir, take a few men and five three-ton vehicles to the ammunition depot and load them with all the ammunition we will require in case of hostilities.'

Always eager to complete the tasks given to him and full of the *josh* a young Indian Army officer is known for, the second lieutenant answers, 'It will be done at the earliest, sir. I will leave right away.'

Since all the support and heavy weapons have been left behind by the battalion at their previous location in the northeast, Lt Col Kapur immediately writes a DO[4] to his previous Brigade Commander, Brig Chiman Singh, to arrange the weapons on priority. Understanding the magnitude of the situation, Brig Chiman Singh and Capt Sangram Singh – an officer from 1st JAK Rifles who is attached to the Brigade Headquarters as GSO 3 (Intelligence) – ensure that all the weapons the battalion will require are dispatched at the earliest.

Meanwhile, after initial trouble at the ammunition depot, 2nd Lt Jasbir returns with five three-ton vehicles fully loaded with ammunition. It took a stern request, and the 'OP IMMEDIATE' indent drafted by the unit Quartermaster, Capt Balwant Singh, to convince the Commandant of the depot to arrange all the ammunition at the earliest.

Finally, after days of anxious waiting, the 1st JAK Rifles is moved to the border in a long convoy formed out of military trucks, Army Jeeps and a few civilian vehicles. The soft-spoken Dogra troops merrily talk among themselves. Some of them fall asleep as the trucks carrying them wade their way through the uneven road.

During the long journey, Lt Col Kapur's thoughts involuntarily drift away to his family far away in Delhi. He last saw them five months ago when he was in Delhi for official work. With the ongoing friction at the East Pakistan border, he is sure that he will not see them again for a minimum of six to eight months.

---

4 Demi Official letter. Generally used in correspondence between government officers for inviting their personal attention on the issue.

He can't help but reminisce the time he spent with his family. His school-going children – a son aged ten, and a daughter aged eight – made the most of his brief stay at home. They made sure that he played with them when they returned from school every day. Mrs Kapur, his wife, who worked at Hotel Oberoi, watched them in contentment as her children spent precious time with their father. She knew these moments were rare, as her husband was away for most of the year. Lt Col Kapur was missing a sizeable chunk of his children's growth.

But before he can dwell on it more, he shakes his head and thinks of the deployment of his troops once they reach the border.

THE MUKTI BAHINI

Following the move to the border, Lt Col Kapur deployed all his troops in company groups at important locations. The forward-most company was deployed at Boyra, a strategic location projecting into East Pakistan like a dagger. On the grim occasion that the situation worsened in the future, it was from Boyra that the Indian Army would launch forays into enemy territory. Hence, occupying Boyra and keeping it a stronghold of the Indian Army was a no-brainer for the 1st JAK Rifles.

The battalion headquarters along with the Alpha Company, led by the enterprising Maj Harish Pant, were established at Duttapulia, at a considerable distance from the border. Close to the battalion headquarters was a camp housing refugees who had escaped the wrath and atrocities of West Pakistan's army and fled from their own country to the neighbouring West Bengal. Amongst the refugees were people who had resigned from their jobs – defence service officers, JCOs and other ranks – who wanted to fight against the much-dreaded enemy army.

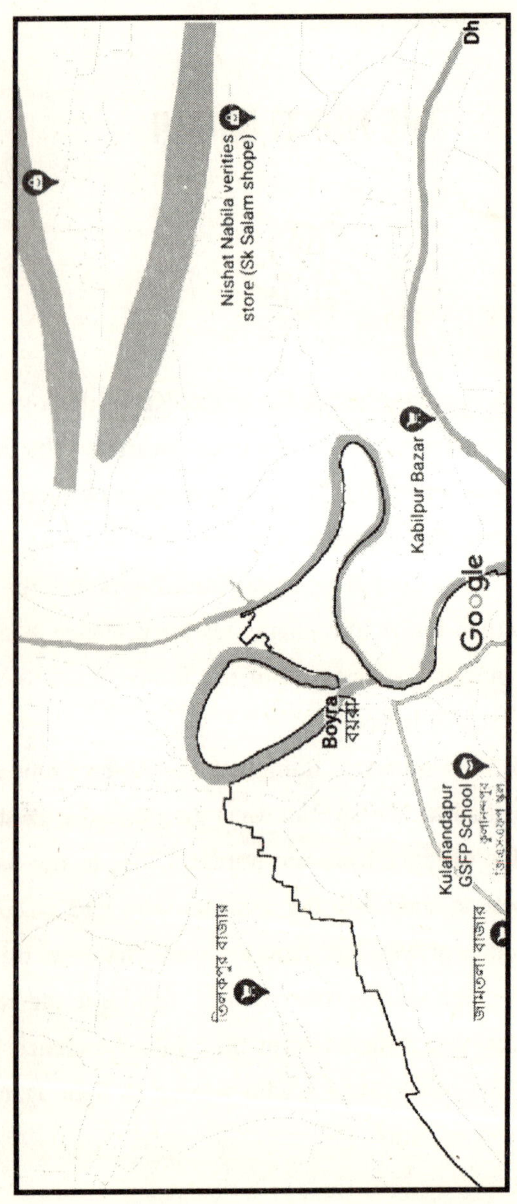

Present Day Boyra: Projecting into Bangladesh like a Dagger

One day, while passing by the camp, Lt Col Kapur came across the pitiful condition of the refugees. He felt a sense of melancholy. All these refugees were living a peaceful and prosperous life with their families in their homeland just a month ago. Under *Operation Searchlight*, a crackdown engineered by the West Pakistani army, their homes and existent peace had been destroyed. The women of their house had been kidnapped, raped, or murdered. Many of these refugees had lost their fathers, sons, or brothers to the bloodthirsty Punjabi soldiers of West Pakistan.

As he walked past them slowly, contemplating, Lt Col Kapur was pleasantly surprised to see a boy, about five, standing up and saluting him crisply. A bright smile lit up the boy's face as his salute was acknowledged by the Colonel. Turning to Subedar Major Sadhu Singh, who was walking just behind, Lt Col Kapur asked with marked concern, '*Sahab*, do you know who this boy is? Is he also a part of the refugees?'

Sounding sombre, the Sub Maj said, 'Yes sir, I know this boy. He stays here at the camp with his old and weak grandfather.'

Turning back to look at the boy again, Lt Col Kapur asked further, 'What about the others from his family?'

With a sad look on his face, the Sub Maj said, 'Sir, his father has been beheaded by West Pakistan's army, and his mother and grandmother have been taken away by the marauders. I shudder to think what they must have done to those poor creatures. He fled his home with his grandfather with great difficulty.'

Adding more, he continued, 'Just a few days back, he did not even have the strength to stand.'

Almost immediately, Lt Col Kapur enquired, 'Then?'

'Our mess cook sympathized with him, and along with a few of our boys, carried a few mess tins filled with rice and daal for him and his grandfather,' said Sadhu Singh.

Mightily impressed with his boys, Lt Col Kapur beamed, 'Great. The little nutrition we provided has brought the boy back to his feet.'

Soon, many of the refugees, most of them who had earlier been a part of Pakistan's army, formed a force known as the Mukti Bahini. A huge chunk of this force comprised Bengali Muslims, with a few Bengali Hindus contributing to the ranks as well. The 1st JAK Rifles and the other battalions posted at the border had been tasked by the higher-ups to train the Mukti Bahini personnel and sieve them into cohesive fighting units.

To train the Mukti Bahini in minor battle tactics and in the use of rifles, grenades and mines, Lt Col Kapur appointed Lt Shashi Bahl as an instructor. Lt Bahl was a bright young officer who was among the fittest men in the battalion. At a training camp at Chakulia, under his supervision, the Mukti Bahini personnel considerably improved their firing and other soldierly skills. He also trained them in commando type special missions to be carried out behind enemy lines.

The higher-ups had advised the battalions to guide Mukti Bahini to sabotage the fighting capabilities of the enemy. One of their major goals was to lure Pakistan's army in East Pakistan to expending its ammunition, which was already in short supply. Replenishing it from West Pakistan would be a Herculean task.

The onset of the monsoon months completely halted the training and other activities of the Mukti Bahini. The riverine terrain in the region added to the misery, as most of the roads and fields were fully flooded. To make matters worse, the roads leading to other rifle companies from the battalion headquarters were submerged under four feet of water and the fields on either side of the road were submerged eight feet under water. Luckily enough, the roads connecting the Brigade and division to the battalion remained motorable. Two boats with outboard motors, allocated to the battalion, were used to transport ration and mail to the forward companies.

As the monsoon reached its peak, several refugees moved into the battalion headquarters and there was a constraint on the already sparse accommodation facilities. One evening, when the water level at the headquarters rose more than normal, Lt Col Kapur asked the Sub Maj to take four strong soldiers and lift the statue of Lord Krishna, placed on a two-and-a-half-foot high platform, and dip its feet in the water.

Much to the surprise of everyone, the water level did not rise again and started to recede by the next morning. Over the next eight days, the water level decreased considerably and the roads to the rifle companies were again motorable. The reduction in water levels immediately after the lord's feet had been dipped in the water was seen as a miracle. The highly religious troops of 1st JAK Rifles were assured that god's hand was on them and that in case a war broke out soon, they would emerge victorious

As soon as the monsoon subsided, the activities of the Mukti Bahini began in real earnest. Capt Najmul Huda, a former ASC officer in the Pakistan army and twenty-five other ranks constituted the first group of the Mukti Bahini, which was ready for operations. They were detailed to operate under the guidance of 1st JAK Rifles and cause havoc among the enemy. The officers and men of the 1st JAK Rifles trained the Mukti Bahini in using mines, especially the trip wire mines.

The trip wire mines had a very thin metal wire, almost invisible from far, attached to the mine. Once the mine was planted, the wire was tied to a nearby peg. If the wire was pulled by an accidental touch of the advancing enemy, the mine jumped to a height of four feet and blasted, sending metal splinters all around, much like a grenade. The Mukti Bahini was trained to plant these mines with a long trip wire so that they could manually pull it once the enemy troops came within the range of the mine.

Thereafter, on numerous occasions, the Mukti Bahini inflicted sizeable casualties on the West Pakistan army with the use of manually pulled trip wire mines. The sudden blast and the intense firing from the Mukti Bahini which followed, put a dampener on the spirits of the enemy. They started living with the constant fear of mine blasts and sudden ambushes by the Mukti Bahini. A few of their tanks had also been destroyed by the anti-tank mines, which had been carefully laid in their tracks. The enemy casualties reduced gradually, as they were more alert to the danger. But the fear, phobia and apprehension that had been instilled in them was something the Indian Army wanted to achieve before the actual war.

One morning, while Lt Col Kapur was overseeing the preparations of his troops, Capt Najmul Huda arrived rather excitedly and reported to him at the firing range. Unable to contain the excitement for long, Capt Huda informed, 'Sir, the new Bangladesh flag has been designed and is now under production. Very shortly, we will have our own flag.'

Pleased at this development, Lt Col Kapur said, 'Many congratulations on the new flag, Captain. We will do everything possible to help you hoist it on your own land.'

'Thank you, sir,' acknowledged the Captain.

After a short pause, Lt Col Kapur thoughtfully said, 'Why don't you get a handful of two-feet by three-feet flags once they are ready?'

'I will surely get them, sir, but what will you do with so many of them?' asked the Captain rather cheekily.

Grinning from ear to ear, Lt Col Kapur remarked, 'Wait and watch, my friend.'

A few days later, Capt Najmul Huda and a few of his men reported to the battalion headquarters, bringing along with them a few newly-made Bangladesh flags. Following a brief exchange of the latest updates, Lt Col Kapur led Capt Huda and his men to the location of the Charlie Company, led by the daring Maj Harnam Billawaria. After taking a report of the activities from his Company Commander,

Lt Col Kapur and Capt Huda came to a vantage point from where the closest enemy posts were visible.

Pointing his finger at a faraway concentration of brick houses and bunkers around eight hundred metres away, Lt Col Kapur asked, 'Captain, can you see the Pakistani post there?'

Straining his eyes slightly to look ahead, Capt Huda said, 'Yes sir, I can see that post. It looks as though it is very strongly held.'

'Yes, it is. We must somehow lower their morale,' said the Colonel, still looking at the post.

With an ambiguous look on his face, Capt Huda asked, 'But how, sir? Your country hasn't declared war yet and we, the Mukti Bahini, are still not capable enough to capture such a fortified area.'

Paying little heed to the concerns of the Captain, Lt Col Kapur again asked, 'Do you see that tree there? The one which is around a hundred metres ahead of their post?'

'Yes sir, I do,' confirmed the captain.

Fixing his eyes with those of Capt Huda, Lt Col Kapur, said, 'Why don't you take a few of your boys tonight and put up a Bangladesh flag on that tree?'

Taken aback, Capt Huda pleaded, 'But why? If they catch us, we will be slaughtered. It is very dangerous.'

Breaking into a loud laugh, Lt Col Kapur said, 'Don't worry, young man. The Pakistanis are off guard at night. If anything happens, we will support you. Just plant a flag on that tree and retreat quickly.'

Realizing that the CO of the 1st JAK Rifles must have made a crafty plan, Capt Huda agreed and walked away without more prodding. He had been with the Colonel long enough to understand that he would not risk the lives of the men under his command unnecessarily. He also knew that millions like him dreamt of forming a separate country and that was only possible with the support of the Indian Army.

A while after the Mukti Bahini personnel had left, Lt Col Kapur moved to the Medium Machine Gun (MMG) nest of the Charlie Company and ordered the soldiers manning it, 'Aim your MMG on that tree there. Once the enemy soldiers realize that the Mukti Bahini has planted its flag on their territory, I am sure they will try to remove it. If they attack the Mukti Bahini, defend them.'

The next morning, much to their frustration and anger, the Pakistanis spotted the newly-made Bangladesh flag on the tree ahead of their post.

Pleased by the results, the Mukti Bahini troops planted more such flags near Pakistani posts and on many likely routes taken by Pakistani convoys. The activities of the Mukti Bahini achieved their aim – they dented the morale of the Pakistan army. However, to completely dislodge them from their strong perch, a killer blow from the Indian Army was required.

SKIRMISH AT BOYRA

The war clouds started gathering swiftly by the end of October 1971, and it was now only a matter of time before the first bullets would be fired. Realizing the need for his boys to be motivated and ready to face the war, Lt Col Kapur put them under a rigorous training schedule. To instil in them the sacred values of *naam, namak* and *nishaan,*[5] he told them about the history of 1st JAK Rifles and how its erstwhile officers and men had given their blood and sweat to emerge victorious in battles of the past.

To ensure that there were no loose ends when the war broke out, Lt Col Kapur and the officers and men from his 'R'[6] group carried out a thorough reconnaissance of the enemy defences opposite them. From a vantage point atop a tree on own side, Lt Col Kapur could clearly see the enemy troops going about their routine in a mundane manner. He could see some of them bathing in the nearby Kabadak

5 *Naam* is the name of the regiment and battalion. *Namak* is for the salt the men have eaten during their service in the battalion. *Nishaan* is the symbol/colours/crest of the regiment.

6 A small group of officers and men from the battalion who carry out the reconnaissance of enemy defences before an attack.

River and others carrying some heavy weapons to the posts. Many of them, he saw, were strengthening their defence, both temporary and permanent.

'Gentlemen, the enemy seems prepared for the upcoming war. I hope your respective companies are ready for action?' Lt Col Kapur asked his company commanders in the operations room once they returned from the reconnaissance.

'They are absolutely ready and raring to go, sir,' assured Maj Harnam Billawaria, the Charlie Company Commander. From what he had seen over the last year-and-a-half, Lt Col Kapur knew that Maj Billawaria was one of his most bankable officers. He had proved to be an extremely efficient leader under trying circumstances in the past.

The Alpha Company Commander, Maj Harish Pant, and the Bravo Company Commander, Maj K.K. Khajuria, also confirmed that their men were ready. The Delta Company Commander, Maj Sarwan Singh, a top-notch boxer, said in his typical style, 'Sir, my boys are ready to give the enemy a bloody nose.'

Pleased by their responses, Lt Col Kapur turned to his IO (Intelligence Officer), 2nd Lt Umesh Gupta, 'Summon the men from your intelligence section immediately. We need to construct a detailed sand model of the enemy positions facing us.'

THE FIRST FACE-OFF

On 3 November, when most of the battalion was concentrated closer to the battalion headquarters to take part in pre-war training, they heard the sound of gunfire at a distance. Certain that the firing was from somewhere close to their own border defences, Lt Col Kapur ordered all his men to rush back to their company defences to meet any contingency. Even though he was slightly perturbed, he knew the skeleton force he had left behind to man the defences was capable of handling any eventuality.

On his way to the defences, Lt Col Kapur ran into Mukti Bahini personnel, who seemed to be gasping for breath. Getting hold of a few of them, Lt Col Kapur asked, 'Where are you running back from? What's the firing all about?'

'Sir, we had gone close to the Pakistan outpost at Maslia and fired at them. They reacted sharply and started chasing us,' said one of them, 'but we have somehow managed to survive. They are now closing in on your defences.'

As soon as Lt Col Kapur heard of the advancing enemy, he and his men sprinted to the Bravo Company without wasting any time. That was where the firing was most intense. The sight of his men firing back aggressively with their machine guns and personal carbines brought a smile to his face. The dogged defence they displayed pleased him. Two enemy platoons had advanced in extended line formation, crossed the International Border (IB) and come very close to the Bravo Company positions. The disciplined fire of his soldiers halted the enemy attacking force in its tracks.

Keen to maintain the momentum, Lt Col Kapur tasked twenty of his men to outflank the enemy and ordered them to either kill or capture the attackers. Completely stunned by the aggressive return of fire and the threat of the outflanking column, the Pakistani soldiers fled back to their post in haste, leaving behind a few of their dead.

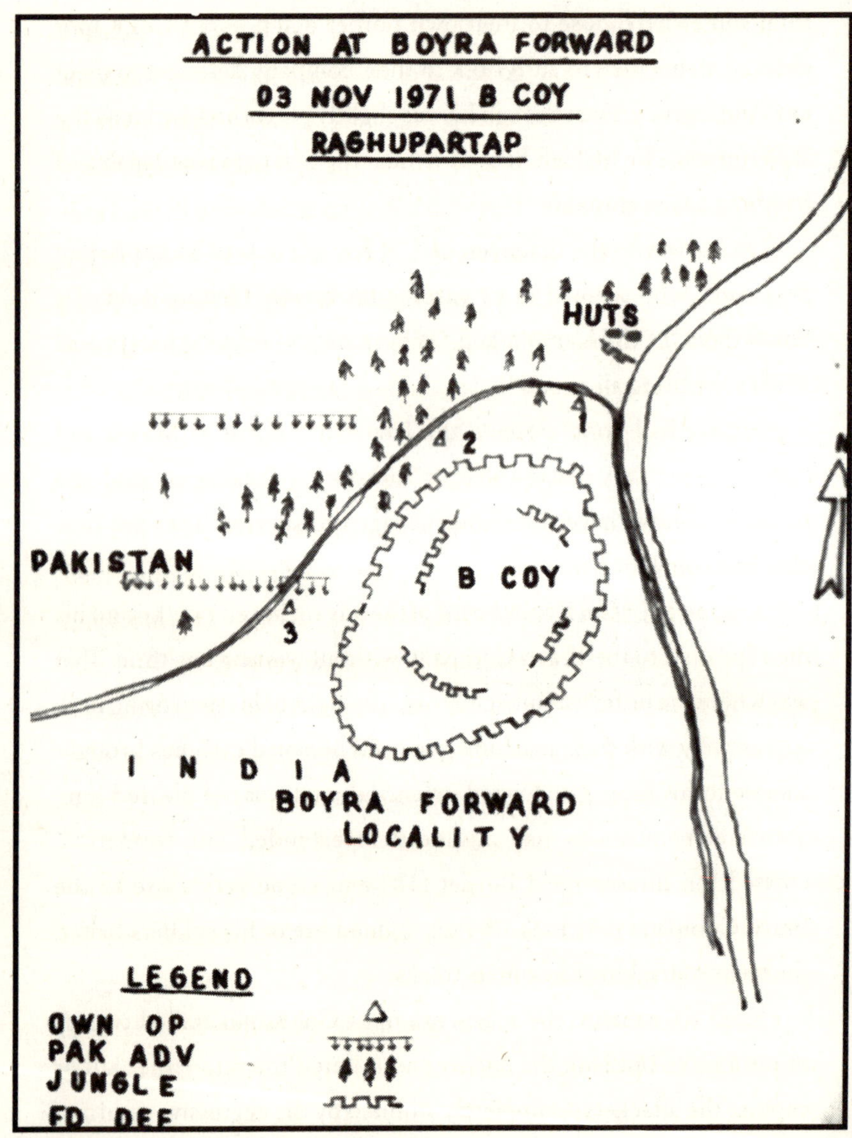

Action at Boyra Forward

To ascertain the identity of the enemy, Lt Col Kapur dispatched a platoon strength patrol to go ahead of the Bravo Company positions and find clues about the enemy that had attacked them. After a thorough search of the area, the patrol returned with three enemy dead bodies and three Chinese rifles with bayonets attached to them. From the identity and service cards found on them, it was confirmed that the dead soldiers were from the 6 Punjab (Pakistan) and 3 Frontier Force (FF) battalions of the regular Pakistan Army, and not the Pakistan Rangers who usually controlled the Indian border with Pakistan.

The next morning, Lt Gen T.N. Raina, MVC, the GOC of 2 Corps, and Maj Gen Dalbir Singh, the GOC of 9 Infantry Division, came to the Boyra forward location to take stock of the situation. After hearing what had transpired the previous day, they were mightily impressed and congratulated the battalion for its prompt actions. Lt Col Kapur, Maj Khajuria and the personnel of Bravo Company received special praise. The advance by the enemy was seen as an attack on our post – an act of war. In addition, the presence of soldiers from the regular Pakistan army instead of Pakistan Rangers so close to the border was enough to indicate that they were gearing up for war.

'Be ready for any offensive in East Pakistan, Colonel. Your orders will come soon,' said Lt Gen Raina, with fierce determination in his eyes. He knew more than a thing or two about war, as he was a highly decorated officer who had seen action many times over his long and storied career. His Corps – 2 Corps – had been assigned the task of meeting the challenges posed by the enemy in the south-western sector of East Pakistan.

III

THE BATTLE OF MASLIA

On the morning of 11 November, Lt Col Kapur was at the battalion headquarters, reviewing the situation, when he was summoned to the Brigade headquarters. Once he got there, Brig H.S. Sandhu, the Brigade Commander of 350 Infantry Brigade, passed the much-awaited orders.

'Surinder, I want your unit to capture the enemy outpost at Maslia tomorrow night. It is going to be our first offensive in the south-western sector of East Pakistan,' said the well-built Brigadier.

With a twinkle in his eye, Lt Col Kapur said, 'The post will be captured at all costs, sir. 1st JAK Rifles will not disappoint you.'

Rushing back to his battalion headquarters, Lt Col Kapur ordered all his officers to assemble in the operational room for an urgent briefing. As he was enjoying some piping hot tea, perfect to tackle the unforgiving winter, Lt Col Kapur asked 2nd Lt Umesh Gupta and a few of his men to uncover the sand model and prepare it for the briefing. Within the next hour, all the Company and Platoon Commanders trickled in slowly from their respective locations and took their seats around the sand model.

'Gentlemen, we have been ordered to capture the enemy outpost at Maslia tomorrow night,' the Colonel began, pointing his cane stick at the small red squares on the model depicting the enemy bunkers at Maslia.

Once the excitement of going to war among his officers settled down, he continued, 'The Alpha and Delta Companies will attack the post frontally from the south-western direction, while the Bravo Company will stay at the Boyra forward area as a reserve.'

Placing his stick over a light blue area on the map, he added, 'This is the fast-flowing and narrow Kabadak River. While the enemy is on its western bank, the eastern bank is unmanned. Maj Harnam, I want you to lead your Charlie Company along the unguarded eastern bank and then cross over to the western bank at Digalsingha to establish a block behind the enemy post.'

Unable to hold on to his excitement, Maj Harnam said, 'To kill the retreating enemy.'

'You are right,' chuckled his CO.

'Boats have been arranged for the Charlie Company to cross the river safely,' added 2nd Lt Umesh Gupta.

Putting his stick down, Lt Col Kapur said, 'To support our attack, the Mukti Bahini personnel will take up positions to the west of the enemy and put in a feint attack ten minutes before H-Hour[7].'

2200 Hrs, 12 November 1971

It's a bitterly chilly night, but it does not matter. The assaulting troops from the Alpha and Delta Companies swiftly move in the dark

7 The time an attack is to be launched. It's called the 'Hotel Hour' or H-Hour.

towards the Forming-Up-Place (FUP), approximately 400 metres from the enemy post, to launch the attack by 2300 hrs. All they can see in the darkness is the outline of the enemy bunkers they have been tasked to attack and clear tonight. With only an hour to go, they push against the strong and rough wind and finally take up positions, waiting anxiously for the order to attack.

It is at this moment that Lt Col Kapur, who is right behind the assaulting troops, receives a call from the Brigade Headquarters. He is told to abort the attack. Frustrated at the last minute command, he asks, 'May I know why the attack has to be aborted?'

Brig Sandhu says, 'The higher-ups have other plans on their mind. We must do what we are told.'

Still disappointed, Lt Col Kapur again asks, 'What is my battalion supposed to do now?'

'Prepare and dig your defences at the FUP. Simulate feint attacks on the enemy and make them expend their ammunition,' orders the Brigadier.

The message is passed and carried out. As per the earlier plan, the same night, the Mukti Bahini puts in a feint attack on the enemy from the western flank and makes it expend its ammunition. Similarly, the Alpha and Delta Companies also fire at the enemy and shout the regimental war cry of '*Durga mata ki jai!*'

The enemy is under the illusion that it is under attack and fires from all cylinders. Strings of enemy machine gun fire hit the stonewalls and large trees behind which the men of 1st JAK Rifles have taken cover. Barks of tree trunks are peppered with a heavy volume of Pakistani machine gun fire, but not a single defending soldier is hurt. They watch in amusement as the Pakistani soldiers expend their ammunition mindlessly.

To further deceive the enemy, having judged the direction of the wind, Lt Col Kapur orders his men to fire the 2-inch parachute bombs. Once the bombs are dropped, the parachutes, owing to the strong breeze, sail back towards the positions of 1st JAK Rifles, thus causing the shadows of nearby trees to move towards the enemy. The Pakistan Army mistakes the moving shadows of the trees as an attack by the advancing Indian soldiers and they fire continuously to 'beat back' the attack. The hardy Dogras chuckle merrily as they watch their enemy wasting his ammunition blindly.

Meanwhile, in the dead of the night, Maj Harnam skilfully leads his men along the eastern bank of the Kabadak, avoiding enemy detection. He lets his thoughts briefly drift away to his family. The last time he had been home, his wife was heavily pregnant, carrying their first child. Bidding her goodbye and heading to a potentially warlike situation had been extremely difficult. He wanted to be by her side, but here he was, leading a mission behind enemy lines. He forces his mind to return to the present.

Maj Harnam and his men reach the exact location from where they are to cross over to the other bank. The first boatload comprises fifteen odd men, led by the recently-promoted Naib Subedar Sukhdev Singh. The men are halfway across the narrow river, when, by sheer bad luck, an enemy patrol comes up on the other side of the bank and starts questioning the identity of the members on the boat.

Getting no answer, the suspicious enemy troops, who do not want to take any chances in the dark, fire a few shots at the boat. One of the bullets punctures the boat and panic sets in. Realizing that his man will be shot to pieces if he does not act fast, the brave Sukhdev Singh orders them to lie down and paddle the water with their hands until they reach the eastern bank again. The enemy troops, who are just forty metres away, fire violently, but they miss their targets. It is too dark to aim properly.

Once near the safe bank, Naib Subedar Sukhdev Singh gets into the waist-deep freezing water and orders his men to jump onto the bank one at a time. To cover their move and to prevent the enemy from taking potshots at them, he takes charge of the Light Machine Gun (LMG) and suppresses the enemy. It is largely because of his heroics that not a single man from his platoon is killed.

Meanwhile, Maj Harnam receives orders that the attack has been aborted and that he should return to base with all his men. 'Sir, it's almost daylight and I can roughly see four enemy trucks parked almost 800 metres away from my position. Troops can be seen alighting from it with an intention to attack us,' says Maj Harnam.

Sighing, Col Kapur orders, 'Okay, Harnam. I leave it to you. Either return using fire and move or stave off the enemy attacks and then return.'

'I prefer the latter, sir,' pats back the enthusiastic Major.

'You have the Artillery Forward Observation Officer (FOO) with you. Make use of Arty fire to break the enemy attacks,' advises Col Kapur.

The enemy puts in three strong attacks on Maj Harnam and his company troops, but fails to make any gains. Maj Harnam, co-ordinating with the Battery Commander Maj Mishra, brings down accurate artillery fire on the enemy. Heavy casualties are inflicted on the enemy and the day is saved. On hearing that the enemy attacks have been broken, Lt Col Kapur orders Maj Harnam to bring his men back to the base at Boyra for further orders.

On return to Boyra, Maj Harnam receives a telegram from home announcing the birth of his son! It's a moment to doubly delight and he celebrates his victory over the enemy and the birth of his son amidst his brave men. The men are extremely happy for their sahab and take turns in giving him a warm hug.

On the evening of 13 November, the Alpha and Delta companies strengthen their defences, opposite the enemy post at Maslia, with overhead fortifications. Guided by their able CO, the men make good use of both man-made and natural cover. Sandbags and huge stones found nearby are used to make sangar[8]-like structures. Many men also take cover behind the trees and await the impending enemy response.

---

8 A sangar is a man-made defensive structure made out of loose rocks and stones. It can accommodate 2-5 men depending on its size and shape.

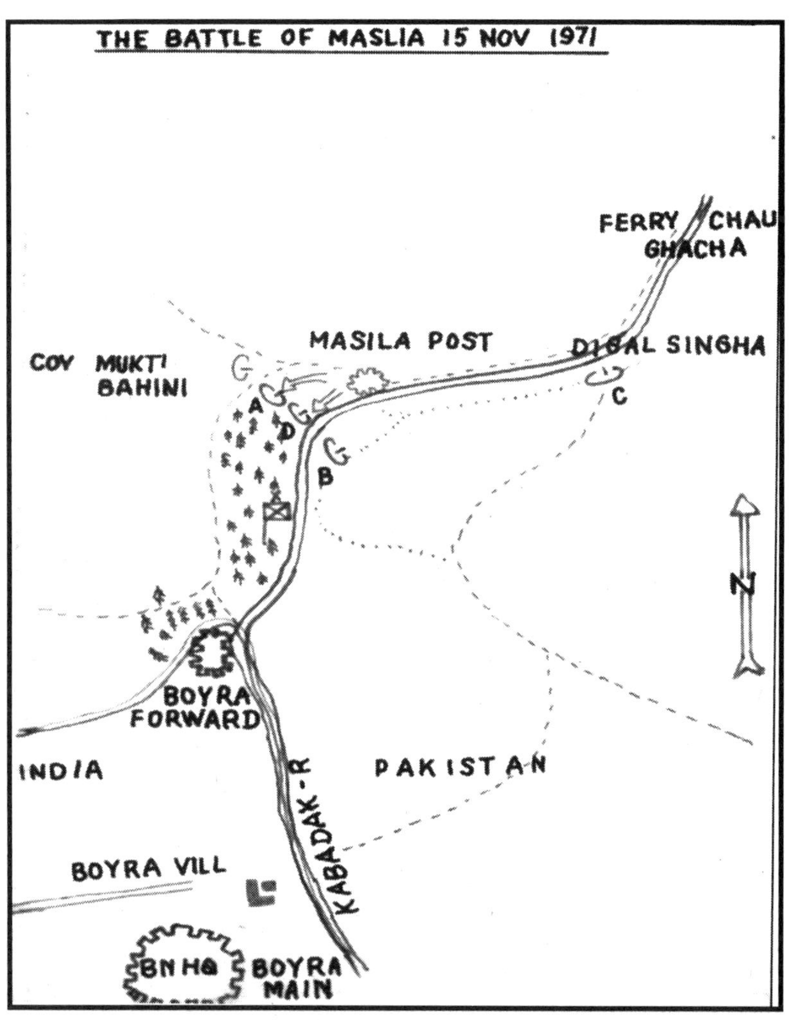

The Battle of Maslia

The Bravo Company is asked to come upwards from Boyra and take defences in line with the other two forward companies. To ensure that the enemy is taken by surprise, Lt Col Kapur orders the Bravo Company to stay linear to the other two companies but to take up defences on the other bank of the Kabadak River so that the enemy's attention is diverted. Followed by a well-deserved day of rest, the Charlie Company under the gallant Maj Harnam is ordered to move out of Boyra and provide depth to the defences.

Before sunrise on 14 November, all fighting personnel of the 1st JAK Rifles take up positions inside enemy territory, becoming one of the first battalions of the Indian Army to enter East Pakistan! The defence of Boyra is handed over to another great battalion, 14 Punjab.

During the day, locals friendly to the enemy are captured by the forward troops and handed over to the Mukti Bahini for further interrogation and disposal. It is revealed that they were ordered by the enemy commander at Maslia to ascertain the strength and layout of the Indian defences. Intense patrolling by the enemy is also observed during the night by the vigilant sentries.

At night, accompanied by his IO and Battery Commander (BC), Lt Col Kapur visits all his forward companies. As an enemy attack on them is imminent, he asks them to stay focused. He reminds them of the atrocities committed by the West Pakistan army on the women and children of East Pakistan. He tells them how the refugee crisis in India and the consequent economic burden have been orchestrated by the arrogant West Pakistan army. Finally, he implores them to teach a tough lesson to the over-ambitious and haughty enemy troops.

Lt Col Kapur and Maj Mishra are certain that the enemy attack will be frontal, hence, when they reach the Bravo Company location, Lt Col Kapur takes aside Company Commander Maj Khajuria and the JCOs for a quick briefing.

'Major, I am sure that the enemy will make a frontal assault on the Alpha and Delta Companies,' says the CO. 'I want you to position your MMGs in such a way that they can provide enfilade fire in front of those two company locations. This will ensure that the enemy is caught in a crossfire; escaping which will become impossible.'

To be doubly sure, Lt Col Kapur checks the siting of the MMGs and instructs the crew to open fire the minute the enemy enters their arc. He also ensures that sufficient ammunition boxes and belts are allotted to the Bravo Company. At around 3:00 a.m., he instructs the BC to fire his big guns right ahead of his own defences when the enemy attacks.

Notwithstanding the early morning haze, the enemy, as expected, launches an all-out frontal attack on the positions of the Alpha and Delta Companies exactly at 5:10 a.m. Ten minutes earlier, the troops of 1st JAK Rifles had been heavily shelled by the Pakistani Artillery and 81 mm mortars. The war cry of Allahu-Akbar reverberates in the air as dawn heavily fills the sky. Slowly but steadily, the Pakistani troops, mostly from 6th Punjab and the Frontier Force regiment, menacingly advance to their objectives.

Just as they think that they have got a free run, the enemy soldiers are pounded by the Indian artillery. Deadly shells rain down on them, and their attack formation is broken. On the advice of

Lt Col Kapur, Maj Mishra brings down artillery fire as close as 150 metres ahead of the forward Indian defences. It's a risky move, but Lt Col Kapur is ready to take the calculated risk. The troops of 1st JAK Rifles watch in delight as numerous enemy soldiers are seen falling under the artillery barrage.

The remaining enemy soldiers regroup quickly and make a dash for the outer perimeter of the defences. This is when the MMGs of the Bravo Company pump into action and fire on the left flank of the enemy from over and across the Kabadak River. At the same time, the troops of the forward companies, who have waited for long with their cold fingers on the trigger, aim and shoot at the enemy ahead from behind their cover positions. The enemy is totally foxed and has nowhere to hide. He is being fired upon from three directions incessantly. Lt Col Kapur, who is right at the front, exhorting his men to fight until the end, is happy that his plans have been well executed by his brave men.

Merely twenty minutes after it had begun, the Pakistani attack is called off. They have been crushed by the enormous grit and determination shown by the frontline troops. Asking his men not to let their guard down, Lt Col Kapur instructs Sub Maj Sadhu Singh to replenish the ammunition. The ammunition is brought from Boyra under the Sub Maj and is distributed by the Charlie Company boys who are in reserve.

Forty-five minutes later, the enemy launches a second attack, but it meets the same fate. The troops from 1st JAK Rifles are proving too hot for them to handle. They had expected to run over the defences, but instead they were making hasty retreats, leaving behind their dead comrades and assorted weapons.

The enemy attacks for the third time an hour-and-a-half after the second attack. It is their fiercest attack, but is beaten back primarily due to the heroics of 2nd Lt Umesh Gupta, Naik Rajinder, Naik Inderjit and Lance Naiks Meghraj, Baldev Singh and Magar Singh. If not for these men, the enemy would have made several dents in the Indian defences.

As the bulk of the fighting rages in front of the Alpha and Delta Companies, a commando-type platoon of the enemy breaks away from the main assault column and outflanks the Indian defences to make a dash for the Battalion Tactical Headquarters (Bn Tac Hqrs), which is at the heart of the defences. This spells danger because the full command and control of the battalion lies in the Bn Tac Hqrs.

Realizing the gravity of the situation, 2nd Lt Umesh Gupta gathers a few men from the protection section, and charges at the incoming enemy. His charge is so ferocious that the advancing enemy loses nerve and retreats. Oozing with confidence and courage, the twenty-two-year-old officer chases the retreating enemy and beats the living daylights out of them. Lt Col Kapur watches with pride in his eyes as the young daredevil and his men return after successfully chasing away the enemy.

Around the same time, an enemy shell lands right on a forward LMG post, injuring the crew. Sensing the chance to overrun the post, a section from the Pakistani attacking force menacingly charges at the post. Fully aware that his comrades will be killed if he does not act fact, Lance Naik Magar Singh rushes to the post and picks up the LMG. He then positions himself at a vantage point and brings down effective fire on the advancing enemy.

A couple of enemy soldiers drop dead by Lance Naik Magar's volley of fire and the remaining flee from the scene of action. However, most unfortunately, a freak shell from the enemy artillery lands close by. The splinters from the shell tear into Lance Naik Magar, and kill him instantly. The LMG post is saved, but Lance Naik Magar Singh will never go back to his home in rural Punjab. Even in death, his fingers are coiled around the trigger of the LMG.

On the flank, commanding the MMG detachment, Naik Rajinder Singh is displaying great battlecraft skills. Being an expert MMG handler, Naik Rajinder Singh directs the right amount of fire on the enemy. During the intense close-range battle, the Pakistani troops focus the bulk of their attention on Naik Rajinder Singh's MMG. They are sure that if the MMG post is destroyed, it will be a huge dent in the Indian defences. Therefore, they incessantly fire at the post and break the firing pin and spare part wallet of the MMG.

The MMG is now nothing but a piece of metal. Under the terrifying sound of shells and bullets, Naik Rajinder Singh decides the next course of action. He sees the enemy is two hundred metres away and slowly progressing. He calculates that it would take them another ten odd minutes to reach the MMG post. Just hundred metres away from Naik Rajinder is another MMG post. He is sure he will find a spare firing pin there. Without further delay, in full view of the enemy, he runs across to the other MMG post. Bullets whiz past him, but fortunately, not even one strikes him.

Naik Rajinder, with the name of Goddess Durga on his lips, fetches the extra firing pin and rushes back to his post just in the nick of time. The enemy is now just fifty metres away. If he follows all the lengthy safety procedures to insert the firing pin, the enemy will surely overrun his post, killing him and his comrades. Hence, on the spur of the moment, he catches hold of the red-hot barrel of the MMG and changes the firing pin. The skin on his hand burns instantly and some of it melts under the immense heat of the barrel.

Naik Rajinder ignores the severe burns on his hand, puts the MMG back in place, and presses the trigger to stall the enemy's advance. Four to five enemy soldiers, who are approaching in a semi-circle, are killed in the very first burst of fire. This breaks the momentum of the assault and the rest of them run back in disarray. Coming from the Kangra Valley in Himachal Pradesh, Naik Rajinder lives up to the rich martial tradition of his forefathers. Blood drips down his hands, but he doesn't bother.

Another hero from the Kangra Valley, Lance Naik Meghraj, rises to the occasion to beat back the waves of enemy attacks. Commanding an LMG detachment, he displays raw courage and tactical acumen of the highest order to confuse the enemy. To surprise the enemy, he picks up the LMG and swiftly changes his position to fire at them. Just minutes later, he again readjusts his position and fires at the enemy from a different direction. The enemy is under the illusion that there are multiple LMGs firing at them, but in actual, it is only

Lance Naik Meghraj who is firing at them from different directions! It is because of such acts of unmatched valour that the third Pakistani attack is also beaten back.

Two more counter attacks follow, but are duly beaten back by the tenacious troops of Raghupratap led by their brave CO, Lt Col Surinder Kapur. Sadly, besides Lance Naik Magar Singh, Naik Inderjit and Lance Naik Baldev Singh are also killed in action. Both the men die gallantly, defending their section positions. Because of such acts of individual and collective valour, the Pakistan army is severely dented and by 10:00 a.m., their fifth and final counterattack is called off.

Making use of the lull, Lt Col Kapur dispatches small patrols to go ahead of the defences for mopping-up operations. Eleven enemy bodies are found lying around in a mangled form ahead of the Alpha Company positions. From the pocket of Maj Anis Ahmed, a Pakistani Company Commander, is found a letter from his brother written in Urdu, which reads, '*Bhaijaan, ab tak aapne kafi dhotiposhan ka khoon chusliya hoga.*' (Dear brother, you must have sucked the blood of many dhoti-clad people by now). This clearly highlights the hate carried by the West Pakistanis against the Bengalis of East Pakistan. Besides these bodies, several high-calibre Pakistani weapons are recovered from the scene of action.

Due to the thick undergrowth ahead of the D Company, only one body, that of a captain, is recovered, along with several assault rifles. It is believed that using advantage of the cover, the enemy had retrieved several of their dead. Six brave hearts of the 1st JAK Rifles lost their lives fighting at Maslia while twenty-two others were wounded.

During the debriefing, some civilians who had carried the Pakistani dead from Maslia to Chaugacha on bullock carts claim that they counted eighty-two Pakistani bodies. When Lt Col Kapur brushes aside their claims, saying that it's too high a number, they vouch they counted the bodies twice and are certain that the number of Pakistani dead is accurate. Hence, enemy casualties during the battle of Maslia are estimated as ninety-four (Twelve recovered by the unit and eighty-two counted by the civilians).

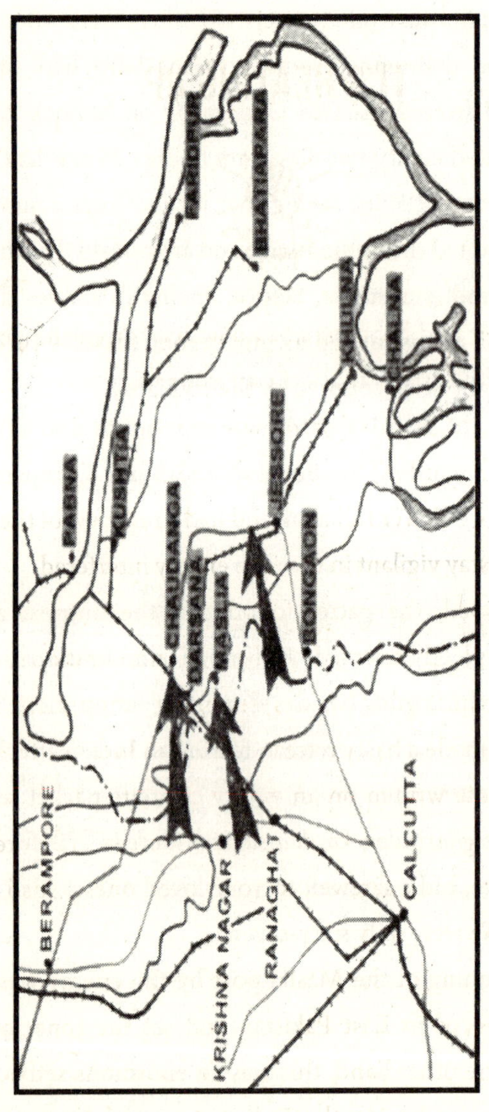

The Map of Maslia

IT'S HEATING UP

Lt Col Kapur and his men saw no activity from the enemy side after the fifth counterattack. Everything had come to a standstill at Maslia. At night, a strong patrol was sent out to find whether the enemy was still guarding the outpost. The Bravo Company was on the eastern bank of River Kabadak and had a full view of the outpost; it was asked to stay vigilant in case the enemy interfered.

As was hoped, the patrol found that the outpost at Maslia had been completely vacated. Half-open ammunition boxes and abandoned machine guns besides dozens of ration sacks indicated the enemy had made a hasty retreat, fearing an Indian attack. During the search, a note written on an empty cigarette packet read, *'Aage badhne se pehle gharwalon ko dua salaam karlena.'* (Before moving ahead from here, bid a farewell to your loved ones.) Also added in English was, 'We were only sixty-seven.'

The abandoning of the Maslia post by the enemy was the first success of 2 Corps in East Pakistan and set the tone for further victories. On the other hand, this was an enormous setback for the Pakistani forces, as having the Indian Army so deep inside their

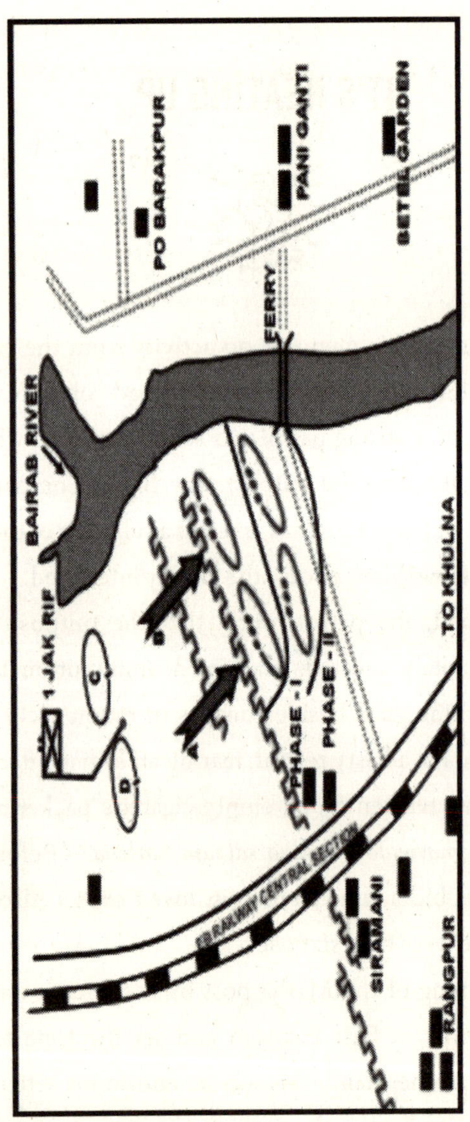

The Map of Syamganj

territory, even before the war had been declared, threatened their strongholds at Jessore and Khulna.

Desperate to dislodge the Indian troops and the Mukti Bahini, Pakistan employed the much dreaded, American built, F-86 Sabre jets from its air force to disrupt the Indian defences. On 17 November, four attempts were made by two sections of Sabre jets to strafe the troops of 1st JAK Rifles with cannons and heavy machine guns, but they failed to achieve their objectives.

Lt Col Kapur, who had craftily deployed his troops using the prominent tree cover and thick foliage to counter the Sabre attack, observed that the Sabre jets were strafing an area considerably ahead and to the left of his defences. This was an expanse, which had fresh signs of digging and was the place from where the Mukti Bahini had carried out its feint diversionary attack a few days earlier. Appropriate camouflage using the vegetation and the absence of enemy ground troops to guide the Pakistan air force saved the 1st JAK Rifles from the mighty Sabres that day.

To further deceive the enemy, Lt Col Kapur sent a platoon under 2nd Lt Jasbir during the night to further dig the place where the Sabres had attacked earlier in the day. This was to give them the impression that the Indian Army was further strengthening its 'defences' in that area. Other platoons were also detailed to carry out similar tasks at safe distances from the battalion defences.

The next morning, Lt Col Kapur sat in his camouflaged 'command bunker', and keenly watched as the enemy Sabre jets flew over his battalion and strafed the places where the digging had been done the previous night. Within minutes, the Sabres flew back to their base at Dacca under the illusion that they had destroyed the Indian defences, whereas not a single scratch had been inflicted on the Indian ground troops!

Meanwhile, a significant battle at Garibpur, nine kilometres inside East Pakistan, on 20-21 November, firmly placed the Indian Army in the ascendancy. The 14th Punjab Battalion (Nabha Akal), with the help of a squadron from the 45th Cavalry, occupied Garibpur and tenaciously beat back an attack from the enemy's 107 Brigade, including infantry and armour columns. The 102 Engineer Regiment, 6 Field Artillery Regiment and 78 Medium Artillery Regiment also played sterling support roles during this battle.

The 14th Punjab lost twenty-eight of its braves, including men like Subedar Malkiat Singh and Naik Piara Singh. Maj Daljit Singh Narag, the bold Sikh officer leading the charge of the Charlie Squadron of 45th Cavalry, lost his life in this battle, but not before he had severely dented the enemy tank and infantry columns. Havaldar Lekh Raj, the Recoilless (RCL) Det Commander, who had single-handedly set ablaze an enemy tank using his RCL gun, came out alive from the battle, despite being under severe danger.

With significant ground lost on both banks of the Kabadak, the Pakistan air force made a very determined attack to dislodge the Indian defences on 22 November. The first two groups of Sabre jets flew over the area with impunity and injured numerous soldiers from 1st JAK Rifles, 4th Sikh and 14th Punjab. One amphibious PT-76 tank from the 45th Cavalry was also knocked out in the Sabre attack.

The Pakistani Sabres now had a clear idea about the layout of the Indian defences. This spelled doom, and unless the Indian Air Force would step in, high casualties were expected.

Around 2:45 p.m. on the same day, four Pakistani Sabre jets menacingly approached the Indian defences for strafing. Unexpectedly and to a loud cheer from the troops of 1st JAK Rifles, four Gnats from the 22nd Squadron of the Indian Air Force intercepted them and engaged in an intense dogfight in the clear blue sky over Boyra. One of the Sabre jets, which had developed engine trouble before the arrival of the Gnats, had veered away, leaving the battle to the other three.

The tiny British-made Folland Gnat aircraft, though agile and quick, was no match for the much superior F-86 Sabre jet, both in size and power. With the acquisition of the Sabre jets, the Pakistani higher command was overconfident that it could blow away the 'tiny' Gnats and rule over the skies. Even though the PAF Sabre jets had been mauled at the hands of the IAF in the 1965 War, they still harped on their superiority in the air, totally discounting the superior skill and bravery of the fighter pilots of the IAF.

Displaying immense guts and exhibiting their skill in handling the joystick to perform highly difficult manoeuvres, the IAF fighter pilots made quick work of the Pakistani jets. Fl Lt Ganapathy accounted for the first Sabre firing his portside auto-cannons accurately on the target. Within seconds of this, Flying Officer Donald Lazarus displayed supreme reflexes, engaged another Sabre, virtually at point blank range, and precisely fired his 30 mm auto-cannons on it. The pilots of the badly hit Sabres ejected, hoping to land among Pakistani ground troops.

The last of the Sabre jets was chased away by Fl Lt Andrew Roy Massey after taking several hits on its body. Billows of smoke could be seen coming out of it as it made its way to Dacca. It was highly doubtful that the jet would be used again. After making a mockery of the much-vaunted Sabre jets in the air battle lasting just three minutes, the four IAF heroes joyfully made their way back to their base at the Dum Dum airport in Calcutta even as the ground troops cheered and clapped for them. While Massey, Ganapathy and Lazarus had secured hits on the Sabres, Flying Officer Soarez had played an equally important role in assisting them. The fighter controller, Flying Officer K.B. Bagchi, had also essayed a crucial role in spotting the enemy jets using his radars.

Though the Sabres were shot at a considerable distance from the 1st JAK Rifles positions, Flying Officer Khalil Ahmed, one of the PAF pilots who had ejected, floated towards the battalion pushed by the strong winds. On seeing this, Lt Col Kapur sent a section from the Bravo Company under 2nd Lt Batan Singh to apprehend him. Meanwhile, after successfully landing on a soft patch of grass, Khalil Ahmed pulled out his revolver and entered a hut in the village to escape capture.

Not finding a trace of the ejected pilot, 2nd Lt Batan and his section carried out a thorough search of the village in which he was seen landing. Finally, acting on the clue given by one of the villagers, 2nd Lt Batan and two men from his section barged into the hut where

Khalil Ahmed was hiding. Despite being head and shoulders above 2nd Lt Batan Singh in height, the terrified Khalil Ahmed pushed forward his revolver and said, 'Sir, I was waiting to surrender.' He was, in all probability, the first Prisoner of War (PoW) in the 1971 War. Fl Lt Parvaiz Qureshi, the other PAF pilot who had ejected, was captured by the 4th Sikh battalion. Decades later, he would rise to become the PAF Chief. On interrogation, it was revealed that both the pilots belonged to the 14th Squadron of PAF. This squadron, nicknamed as *The Tail Hunters,* had damaged many static IAF jets at the Kalaikunda base during the 1965 War. Hence, defeating it and capturing its pilots in the air battle of Boyra was sweet revenge for the IAF!

The robust response by the Indian Army at Maslia and Garibpur and the superiority of the IAF pilots over their counterparts in PAF had many national and international repercussions on both sides. Pakistan's President, Gen Yahya Khan, panicked and declared a national emergency in Pakistan. He also complained to the UN Secretary General, U. Thant, about India violating the UN Charter. In India, Prime Minister Mrs Indira Gandhi asserted that India would do everything in its capacity to protect its sovereign interests. Since Pakistan had done nothing to address the exodus of ten million refugees to India from East Pakistan, India had no option but to exercise military power. The refugee crisis had put a strain on Indian resources and with no western superpower willing to help her due to vested interests, a war was on the brink.

SETBACK AT BURINDA

As the 1st JAK Rifles holds ground in the general area of Maslia, the rest of the 9th Infantry Division builds up in and around Boyra, staying inside the Indian Territory. The extensive training and preparations are done with an imminent war on mind. All the units are told that they must be ready to move inside East Pakistan for offensive action very soon. India and Pakistan are all set for their third war within twenty-four years!

Standing around a colourful sand model of East Pakistan, the GOC of 9 Infantry Division, Maj Gen Dalbir Singh, and his staff officers look at the various alternates they can use to launch offensives in East Pakistan. The Commander of 2 Corps, Lt Gen Raina, and the COS Eastern command, Maj Gen J.F.R. Jacob, have earmarked the 9 Infantry Division, to capture the vital towns of Jessore and Khulna, identified as key fortresses by the Pakistan army. The successful capture of Jessore and Khulna will effectively lock Pakistan's 107 Infantry Brigade out of the battle and eventually help in the planned convergence over the Dacca bowl by the Indian forces.

Following careful study and lengthy discussions, it is planned that the main thrust and advance of the 9 Infantry Division will be along the Boyra-Chowgacha-Singhajuli-Jessore axis. This is a long and semi-circuitous route aimed at surprising the Jessore garrison from an unexpected flank. The 1st JAK Rifles is, however, singularly chosen, as a diversionary force to move along the much shorter and frontal Boyra-Jhikargacha-Jessore axis. This route, the enemy is certain, will be used by the Indian Army for its main attack as there is

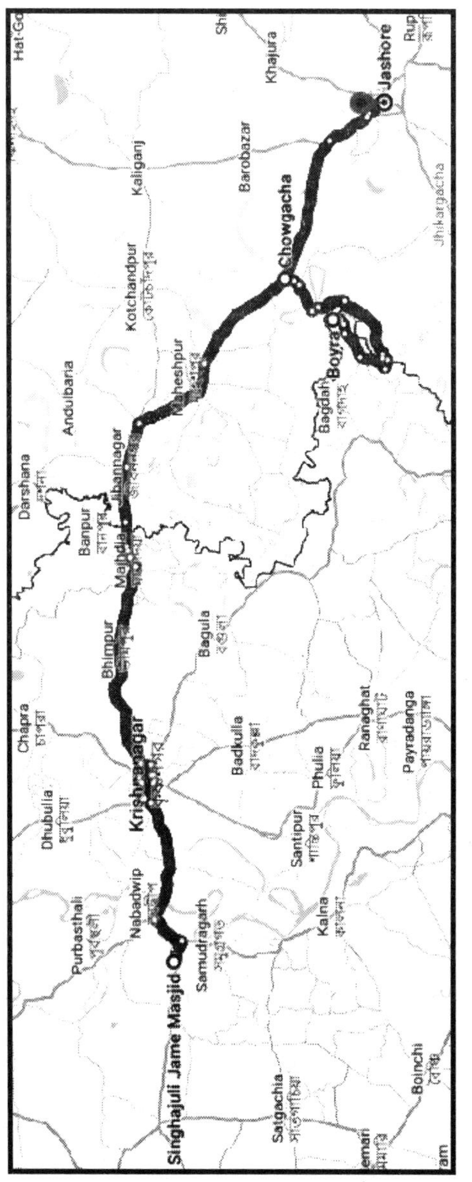

Map highlighting Boyra-Chowgacha-Singhajuli-Jessore axis

a motorable road and railway line from Bangaon on the Indian border to Jessore via Jhikargacha. The total distance is just forty-seven kilometres; much lesser than the actual route chosen by 9 Infantry Division for the main advance.

As per the plan, 1st JAK Rifles is ordered to move from its current location and halt near Mohammadpur. They are tasked with engaging the enemy at Mohammadpur and await further orders. As per inputs from ground intelligence, the enemy troops at Mohammadpur are not more than one company. It is inferred that Mohammadpur is the enemy's delaying position, covering the western approach to their main defence at Jessore.

The next few days are devoid of intense action. Occasionally, the troops of the battalion fire a few rounds at enemy soldiers who carelessly expose themselves. Enemy vehicles that come forward to supply their troops with rations and ammunition are also engaged with mortar and artillery fire. A few patrols are also sent out, but they are asked to be cautious, as there are no orders yet from the higher echelons.

One afternoon, just after he finishes a quick lunch, Lt Col Kapur receives a call from the Brigade Commander. 'Surinder, task a company to clear a standing patrol of the enemy seven hundred metres to the right of Mohammadpur,' orders the Brigadier.

'What's the enemy strength, sir?' asks Lt Col Kapur.

'Not more than two sections,' the Brigadier says confidently.

'But we haven't patrolled that area and neither have we carried a prior reconnaissance,' reasons the CO, his voice dipped with concern.

Brushing aside his concerns, Brig Sandhu says, 'That's not a cause for worry. The enemy's strength is very little. Your men will chase them away.'

Orders are orders. Lt Col Kapur asks Maj Billawaria to clear the enemy 'standing patrol'. Without wasting a moment, all the men from the Charlie Company head towards their assigned objective, led by their valiant JCOs and Company Commander. They weren't ready for this sudden task, but they weren't complaining. This gives them another chance to add glory to the name of their Paltan.

With the western sun kissing them gently, the forward sections inch forward soundlessly to attack the enemy patrol. Gripping their automatic rifles tightly, the brave Dogras dash for the final charge, when bullets and shells rip into them. They are caught in enfilade fire from which there is no escape. Relentless strings of bullets from the enemy MMGs draw blood from the well-built troops of Maj Billawaria's Charlie Company. The attack is stalled. It is now apparent that Maj Billawaria's men are under fire from two enemy companies; one in Burinda and the other in Mohammadpur. Much more than what the Brigade Commander had estimated!

Despite repeated protests by Lt Col Kapur, Brig Sandhu implores him to put in another attack. 'My men will be slaughtered, sir. The enemy is numerically superior,' pleads Lt Col Kapur. 'We have orders from the higher headquarters. The attack must go on,' says the Brigadier before disconnecting. Helpless at his situation, Lt Col Kapur gets in touch with his Company Commander on the radio set and says, 'Harnam, we have been ordered to put in another attack. Go ahead. God be with you.'

With no tinge of hesitance, Maj Billawaria rallies his men and leads another attack. Despite seeing their comrades fall around them, not a single soldier stops. They charge ahead, firing all cylinders and reach very close to the enemy defences.

Pacing up and down his tent, Lt Col Kapur can hear the sounds of intense MMG, LMG, rifle, and mortar fire. He is worried about his men. 'What's the update, Harnam?' he radios his Company Commander. 'We have reached close to the enemy, but have suffered many casualties. My FOO, Capt Sharma, and radio operator, Naik Hari Singh, have been shot badly,' says Maj Billawaria, ducking under enemy bullets.

Realizing that he will lose more men if the attack continues, Lt Col Kapur tells Maj Billawaria to withdraw. With no wireless operator at hand, Maj Billawaria passes on the orders of withdrawal to his Platoon Commanders through word of mouth. It's a sad sight to behold as the Charlie Company boys pick their wounded and dead comrades and retreat from the battlefield.

It has turned completely dark now, but two platoon commanders, Naib Subedar Sukhdev Singh and Sub Raghubir Singh, are not to be found in the camp. They were last seen suppressing the enemy and covering the withdrawal of their men. They simply refused to withdraw! It is later learned that the gallant JCOs had gone down fighting the enemy till their last breath. Naib Subedar Sukhdev Singh, who had proved his worth in the earlier battles, is brought down after he has killed three enemy soldiers.

On the other hand, the highly fit Ghatak platoon commander, Sub Raghubir Singh, is killed after engaging and eliminating multiple enemy soldiers at point blank rage. By bearing the brunt of the enemy fire, they had ensured that others from their platoons survived. Lance Havaldar Krishan Singh is also missing, and it is presumed that he has also died. The completely dark night made it impossible to spot bodies of all the dead soldiers.

'Why did you ask your men to withdraw without my orders?' asks Brig Sandhu, agitated. He has called Lt Col Surinder to his headquarters for debriefing.

'My conscience did not allow me to get my men killed mindlessly,' Lt Col Kapur firmly responds.

'We will have to give this task to another battalion,' declares the Brigadier.

'Please send them in with proper planning and full artillery and armoured support, sir. There are two enemy companies facing us,' suggests Lt Col Kapur, taking a veiled dig at the lack of artillery and armoured support his battalion received for the attack.

Finally relenting and discerning that the attack had been launched hurriedly, Brig Sandhu says, 'I understand where you come from, Surinder. Let your battalion rest for a while and gear up for future offensives.'

WAR DECLARED

On 3 December 1971, fighter jets from the PAF bombed Indian airfields at Jodhpur, Pathankot, Awantipur, Uttarlai, Ambala, Amritsar, Srinagar, and Jaisalmer, among others. Codenamed as Operation Chengiz Khan, these pre-emptive strikes from the PAF were aimed at catching India by surprise. However, the alertness of the Indian forces and inaccurate bombing by the PAF pilots foiled the nefarious designs of Gen Yahya Khan. In retaliation, the Canberra jets of the IAF bombed and struck eight Pakistani airbases.

The same night, Prime Minister Indira Gandhi addressed the nation over All India Radio and made it clear that India would respond with all its might. Months of anticipation and unease had now culminated in a full-blown war. It was time for the Indian Armed Forces to put their training and planning into action.

Following the capture of Burinda by 4 Sikh on 6 December, supported by a squadron of armour and a brigade of artillery, the troops of 1 JAK Rifles noticed that there was no activity on the enemy post at Mohammadpur. A patrol was sent, and it was confirmed that the enemy had withdrawn and only two jackals were seen loitering around.

On receiving the go-ahead from the Brigade Headquarters, Lt Col Kapur assembled his battalion in company columns and ordered them to head for Jhikargacha. Before the move began, a few locals came and informed that Pakistani troops were seen digging the track leading to Jhikargacha. Lt Col Kapur was certain that the digging was done to lay mines and requested the Brigade Headquarters to send engineer support so that the mines could be cleared and the battalion vehicles could move ahead.

Simultaneously, Sub Maj Sadhu Singh was tasked with readying the 'B' Echelon of the battalion for the move. Breakfast was provided to all the troops and lunch packed in their haversacks for consumption at the next stop. There was a loud whisper hanging in the air as the troops had a full breakfast. They were chatting among themselves about the declaration of war and the task their battalion could get in the near future. They harboured in them a sense of revenge for the comrades they lost at Burinda.

Hailing from the plains of Punjab and Jammu, and the mountains of Himachal Pradesh, the troops of 1st JAK Rifles let their thoughts wander back home. For most of them, it had been more than six months from when they were last home. Letters and telegrams had been the only mode of communication with their families. Letters carrying good news had been read by them multiple times. They hoped to finish this war soon and return home safely to see their families again.

After an advance of merely eight hundred metres, a speeding auto rickshaw was seen approaching the forward elements of the battalion. 2nd Lt Umesh Gupta duly halted it and started interrogating the driver. Lt Col Kapur also reached the spot with his party and learned from the driver that the enemy had vacated Jhikargacha and moved back to Jessore in large vehicles.

Not wanting to take any chances, Lt Col Kapur requested if the auto driver could take them to Jhikargacha. The driver immediately agreed and eight men, including Lt Col Kapur, piled up inside the auto! As the auto raced through the countryside, whirring along the river, Lt Col Kapur was trying to find reasons for the enemy's sudden withdrawal. He had never thought that the enemy would vacate Jhikargacha without a fight!

Lt Col Kapur was further surprised when he saw the extent of enemy preparations at Jhikargacha. Right in front and to his left, he saw an extensive ditch-cum-bund running parallel for close to two thousand metres. On his right was the fast-flowing Kabadak River, which had been following them from Boyra. Enemy pillboxes and sangars were seen strung across the entire frontage. This made it certain that the enemy had expected the 9 Infantry Division to approach Jessore via Jhikargacha.

'Capturing Jhikargacha in a battle would have caused us many casualties,' remarked Lt Col Kapur, marvelling at the enemy's defences.

'I agree, sir. But why has the enemy retreated without a fight?' questioned 2nd Lt Umesh. He had used the last eight months to learn a lot from his CO.

'I have no answers, boy. I think the upcoming days will give us a clear picture,' the CO said, his eyes still scanning the erstwhile enemy defences.

Further ahead, Lt Col Kapur saw that the rail-cum-road bridge leading to Jessore has been destroyed and was hanging down from both ends. It was clear the enemy had done it to slow down and hamper the movement of the Indian forces heading for Jessore.

As Lt Col Kapur and his party were surveying the area, the rest of the battalion arrived on foot. The vehicles of the battalion were still at Mohammadpur, waiting for the engineers to clear the mines. Just then, the local leaders and villagers jubilantly greeted Lt Col Kapur and his men, and declared that freedom from the Punjabis of West Pakistan was akin to Eid for them. They insisted that the battalion celebrate and have a meal with them, but Lt Col Kapur politely declined. He assured them he would come back after driving out the enemy from Jessore and the rest of East Pakistan.

Soon after, a man riding leisurely on his motorcycle saw the troops of 1st JAK Rifles and halted. He had come from Jessore and claimed that the city had been abandoned by the Pakistani army the previous night. He swore he had driven around the city with his friend and found no trace of Pakistani soldiers.

Lt Col Kapur believed the man's word and got on his wireless to check the progress of the mine clearing on the Mohammadpur-Jhikargacha road. He was told that it would take a few more hours for the road to be cleared and for all the vehicles to move forward. The Engineer Detachment Commander was advised to check for mines only until thousand metres from the Pakistani defences. This would help in speeding up the operations.

Lt Col Kapur knew that it was a golden opportunity for his battalion to be the first to enter Jessore. He did not want to miss it. He decided not to wait for the vehicles and requested the auto rickshaw driver if he could take him to Jessore. The rickshaw driver was more than happy to help and soon, Lt Col Kapur and a few of his men hopped in for a ride to Jessore and for a shot at history!

Before leaving, Lt Col Kapur tasked the MTO, Capt Rajendra Singh Chauhan, to muster a few vehicles that were available nearby so that the rest of the battalion could also reach Jessore. Instructions were also given to check the progress of the mine clearing. The faster the mines were cleared, the sooner the battalion vehicles could fetch up to ferry the troops.

After a detailed search, Capt Chauhan and the adjutant, Capt Arun, to their dismay, found out that there were a very few vehicles in the town and all of them were low on fuel. Just when the search for finding vehicles was proving to be futile, Capt Chauhan was delighted to spot a large fire engine with a full tank.

He got behind the wheel of the fire engine and loaded a platoon of troops on it. Before long, he caught up with the rickshaw carrying the CO, and announced his arrival with the loud ringing of the bell mounted on the fire engine. Lt Col Kapur was startled to hear the loud sound, but was thoroughly pleased when he turned back to see Capt Chauhan and his platoon following him. The ingenuity and enthusiasm of the young officer highly impressed the CO.

Soon, the peculiar Army convoy of one auto-rickshaw and a fire engine reached the outskirts of Jessore!

The Pakistan army had marked Jessore as one of its key 'fortresses'. It was a very important communication hub and cantonment. The defence of Jessore and another important 'fortress', Khulna, located sixty kilometres south of Jessore had been given to Pakistan's 107 Infantry Brigade commanded by Brig Muhammad Hayat. The capture of Jessore, with no resistance, was a pleasant surprise for the Indian Army. Perhaps the speed of their advance on all the routes had unnerved the enemy.

Half an hour later, the rest of the battalion also married up outside Jessore under the guidance of the dependable Sadhu Singh. They were raring to enter Jessore and see for themselves the disarray caused by the Pakistani withdrawal. They cracked a few jokes at the expense of the Pakistan army and its inability to hold ground for long.

Getting onto his wireless, Lt Col Kapur conveyed a message to Brig Sandhu. 'Sir, 1st JAK Rifles is ready to enter Jessore. The enemy has vacated the town completely.'

The orders he got next were a big dampener. 'Halt your troops, Surinder. The vanguard of our division, 7 Punjab (Mechanized), is just a couple of kilometres away from Jessore on the other axis. I don't want a blue-on-blue situation.'

Disappointment writ all across his face, Lt Col Kapur just said, 'Roger,' and turned off his radio. At the outskirts of Jessore, the battalion halted at a large school building, which had large football and basketball fields. Every soldier in the unit, without exception, was disappointed. They had no other option but to bide their time before further orders came.

Despite being denied the privilege of being the first battalion to enter Jessore, the 1st JAK Rifles became the first battalion to enter the abandoned headquarters of Pakistan's 107 Infantry Brigade. From there was retrieved the name board carrying the names of all 107 Infantry Brigade Commanders till date. It was kept safely so that it could be proudly displayed at the officers' mess of 1st JAK Rifles after the war was over.

The name board carrying the names of all 107 Infantry Brigade Commanders till date

GEARING UP FOR ACTION

Post the capture of Jessore on 7 December, the 9 Infantry Division, barring the 350th Brigade, pursued the enemy till Khulna, which lay sixty kilometres to the South of Jessore. Daulatpur, which lay just outside Khulna, was chosen as the last ground of defence by 107 Infantry Brigade under the astute and courageous, Brig Muhammad Hayat.

Brig Hayat, a decorated officer, was a clever tactician. Very early in the war, he realized that holding onto Jessore would be untenable for his Brigade as the Indian Army was rapidly advancing from all flanks. Staying at Jessore would surely result in all his men being killed. Khulna, he estimated, offered better defence potential, and being a port city, gave the best chance for his troops to escape by the sea route in case things went out of hand.

At Daulatpur, Brig Hayat had skilfully deployed the five battalions under his command. Configuring his defences astride the narrow stretch of railroad Jessore-Khulna, he rested his right flank on the fast flowing and hundred metres wide Bhairab River. His left flank he rested on the swampy marshes outside Khulna. This made outmanoeuvring and outflanking the defences impossible and left frontal attacks as the only option left for the Indian forces.

As a result of Brig Hayat's crafty deployment, five valiant attacks by 8th Madras and 13th Dogra of 32 Infantry Brigade and 19 Maratha Light Infantry (MLI) of 42 Infantry Brigade, were beaten back. Despite losing many of their brave men, these battalions could not capture the enemy positions, and were pinned down by effective fire.

DRAWING UP PLANS

On 13 December, to release the pressure and to launch attacks with fresher troops, Lt Col Kapur was asked to come along the Jessore-Khulna road to meet the Brigade Commander for urgent and important orders. Leaving Jessore with his small party, Lt Col Kapur was all but certain that his battalion would be called upon for action very soon.

Under a cluster of trees near the railway track, on the way to Khulna, Lt Col Kapur met Brigadier Sandhu and Maj Gen Dalbir Singh, GOC 9 Infantry Division. They looked worried, and it seemed as though they had been waiting impatiently for Lt Col Kapur to arrive.

'There are urgent orders for you, Surinder,' began Brig Sandhu, looking worryingly at the CO of 1st JAK Rifles.

'Our battalion is ready for any task, sir,' Lt Col Kapur assured.

'Today, an attack by the boys of 19th MLI was beaten back. This is our sixth attack which has failed,' Brig Sandhu said with a sense of remorse. 'I expect your battalion to fetch up from Jessore and clear the enemy stronghold at Syamganj,' he added.

Lt Col Kapur nodded his head in approval, and there was a gush of blood flowing through his veins. This was the moment he and his boys had waited for. The time had come for them to play a crucial part in the 1971 war. The emotions were running so high that everything around him felt like a blur.

At the end of the short meeting, Maj Gen Dalbir Singh patted Lt Col Kapur on his shoulder and said, 'I have a lot of trust in you and your battalion. I am sure your men will clear Syamganj and open the gates to Khulna.' Thereafter, Maj Gen Dalbir wished luck to his junior commanders and left.

Sometime later, Brig Sandhu and Lt Col Kapur met Lt Col Shamsher Singh, the CO of 19th MLI. The two COs were introduced to each other and Brig Sandhu tasked Lt Col Kapur to take over from 19th MLI and launch an attack on the enemy from their firm base.

'Shamsher, take Surinder to your firm base and brief him about the area. I will meet you both here after an hour.' There was a sense of purpose as Brig Sandhu spoke.

Disagreeing, Lt Col Shamsher asked for more time. 'Two hours are a bare minimum, sir. It will take time to reach my battalion from here.'

Unwilling to waste more time, Brig Sandhu said, 'Okay. Surinder, I want you back here after your reconnaissance in not more than an hour and a half.'

'Roger that, sir.'

On their way to the 19th MLI firm base, Lt Col Kapur and 2nd Lt Umesh Gupta spotted a few bodies of the MLI soldiers lying around in disorder. 'This is not fitting for soldiers who have died for their country,' thought the young subaltern.

2nd Lt Umesh was barely twenty-three, but the uncertainty of life during war times had given him the maturity of a lifetime. He had seen grown-up men weep like children at the death of their comrades. Bullets had flown past him; missing him by inches. He knew he was lucky to survive, but was unsure until when his good luck would last. Death could come at any moment.

Soon, led by Lt Col Shamsher, Lt Col Kapur and his party reached the firm base of 19th MLI. They saw that the brave Maratha boys were stuck in a *paan* plantation, which was approximately 250 metres wide and a 100 metres long. The creepers of the paan plant were wound to ten feet long bamboo staves for stability and support. These bamboo staves were vertically embedded in the sandy ground about one foot from each other.

This made visibility through the paan plantation negligible. The dense coverage of bamboo staves made it a very formidable obstacle to cross while holding a rifle. Even lifting the rifle to fire from the shoulder or hip position was extremely hard. However, these bamboo staves and creepers did not prevent enemy bullets from penetrating and hitting the troops of 19th MLI, who had tried to move ahead.

Ahead of the plantation was open ground extending 250 metres up to the edge of Syamganj village and the outer perimeter of enemy defences. The undergrowth here had been significantly cut to give the enemy a clear view of the advancing troops, thus making it an ideal killing ground for them.

Lt Col Kapur was then taken to a small area, which had a hip high wall and was ten metres long. Crouching behind the wall, Lt Col Kapur peered through his binoculars to look at the enemy defences through a gap in the plantation.

He could clearly see Pakistani soldiers, clad in their khaki uniforms, taking positions inside multi-storied concrete houses, bricked bunkers, and behind large sandbags. From his position, he could only see one enemy MMG, but he was certain that there were more.

To ascertain the strength of the enemy and to locate his heavy weapons, 2nd Lt Umesh was sent among the Maratha troops in the paan plantation and simulate an attack on the enemy. This was to serve the dual purpose of the enemy mindlessly expending his ammunition, and giving away his strength and location.

Taking charge of the Maratha troops, 2nd Lt Umesh instructed them to join him in chanting the Maratha war cry of, '*Shri Chhatrapati Shivaji Maharaj ki jai*,' and then fire a few rounds at the enemy without getting exposed.

These instructions were passed around rather quickly and soon there was a cacophony of the war cry, bullets and shells. Thinking this to be an attack on their positions, the Pakistani soldiers manning the Syamganj defences opened up with all the weapons at their disposal.

This happened for quite a while. The daring 2nd Lt Umesh moved around in the paan plantation and simulated attacks on the enemy from different directions. Lessons learned during the Young Officers course (YO), which he had completed recently, were coming in handy for the youngster.

Gauging the extent and sound of the enemy fire, Lt Col Kapur was certain that a minimum of three enemy HMGs and four enemy MMGs were deployed in the area. It was also clear that the frontage of the enemy extended well beyond the frontage of the paan plantation. It was also observed that the MMG and HMG fire was crisscrossing and covering the whole front.

'This will be one heck of a battle,' Lt Col Kapur thought to himself.

Over his career, he had served at various challenging places under many distinguished officers. Among the officers he had served under, Lt Gen Moti Sagar and Lt Gen Harbaksh Singh had left a huge imprint on him. He remembered how they had taken him under their wings and let him into their military acumen and tact. The lessons of military strategy he had learned from them would help him formulate plans for the upcoming battle.

Just as Lt Col Kapur was immersed in his thoughts, his IO came back after a job well done. 'Umesh, well done, my boy! Your deception of the enemy has helped us immensely. We can now chalk out our plans easily.' The satisfied young officer just smiled back. He could not wait for the battle to begin!

'Col Shamsher, our boys will move in and relive your battalion shortly. Thank you for the help. Your boys fought well,' said Lt Col Kapur appreciating the gallantry of the Maratha troops.

'I hope you get those Pakis nice and proper, Col Kapur. I wish you all the good luck,' said the CO of 19th MLI, before Lt Col Kapur headed back to meet the Brigadier.

Sitting on the edge of his chair, Brig Sandhu asked, 'Are your plans ready, Surinder? I am sure your attack will succeed tomorrow.'

Startled, Lt Col Kapur asked, 'You want us to attack tomorrow?'

'Yes. Tomorrow morning.'

Totally against the idea, Lt Col Kapur immediately disagreed. 'It's impossible, sir. My battalion is still at Jessore and it is already well past sunset. By the time they arrive here, it will be early morning. I can't launch tired troops for a daylight attack.'

'There is pressure from the top,' the Brigadier conceded

'We will attack the day after on 15 December. If we attack tomorrow, the results will not be in our favour.'

Lt Col Kapur stood his ground. He did not want his men to die without being given a proper chance to fight. Memories of Burinda were still fresh in his mind. He was a fatherly figure for them and they banked on him for navigating through the war safely.

Acknowledging the moral courage of Lt Col Kapur and seeing merit in his reasoning, Brig Sandhu pushed the attack by a day. The attack would now happen in the morning on 15 December, a Wednesday!

The D-Day fixed, the two officers went about discussing the attack plans over a small sketch. Both of them appreciated the need for armoured support to destroy enemy HMGs and MMGs, which were housed inside the concrete and brick buildings of Syamganj.

'As artillery support will not be available, we will need a squadron of PT-76 amphibious tanks to cross the Bhairab River and give us covering fire,' asserted Lt Col Kapur.

'I totally agree, Surinder. I will try to get you the support of a squadron of PT-76 tanks,' assured Brig Sandhu before leaving.

Shortly after the meeting, as Lt Col Kapur sat fine-tuning his plans, he again got a call from Brig Sandhu. 'I can just give you a troop of PT-76 amphibious tanks, Surinder. Speak to the troop commander and coordinate your plans.'

Disappointed but ready to fight with what he had, Lt Col Kapur crisply said, 'Victory will be ours, sir. Jai Hind!'

The same night, Lt Col Kapur ordered 2nd Lt Umesh to go to Jessore to guide the battalion to the attack area. The march was to be led by the Alpha Company, which would be the right forward company for the attack. Bravo Company, which was earmarked as the left forward company for the attack, would march next. These would be followed by the Delta and Charlie Companies, respectively; the designated reserves for the attack. 2nd Lt Umesh was also told to warn the 'O' group that their orders will be given an hour after they have reached their location.

The battalion Second-in-command (2-IC), Maj S.B. Singh, led the 'O' group and reached Lt Col Kapur's location by late night. With

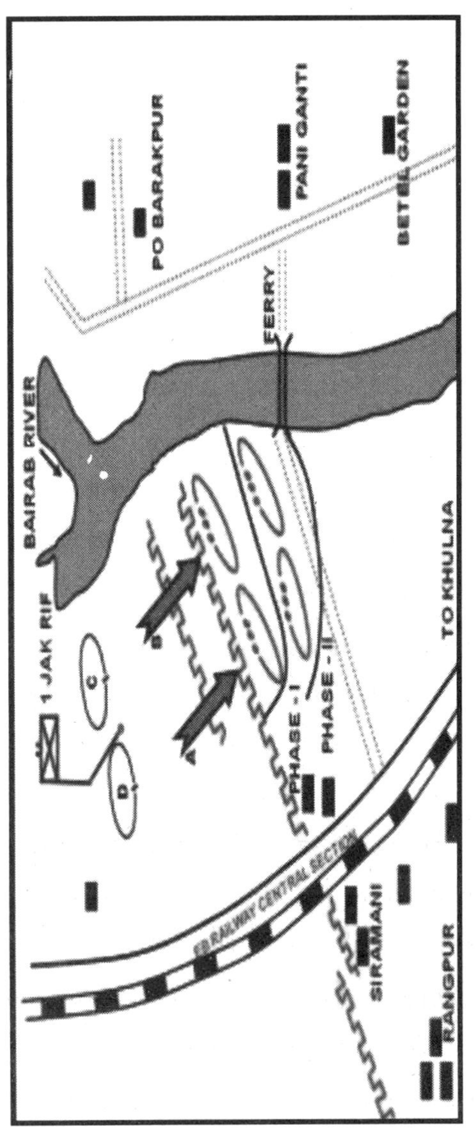

The Map of Syamganj

hot mugs of tea in their hands, the officers and JCOs were briefed by their Commanding Officer in his tent. The clarity with which he spoke left no doubts in their minds that the battalion would succeed.

The broad outline for the attack was as follows:

- The Alpha Company under Maj Harish Pant was to lead the attack from the right flank and capture enemy defences on the right in the first phase of the attack.
- During the same phase, the Bravo Company under Maj K.K Khajuria was to attack from the left flank and capture enemy defences on the left.
- The Charlie Company under Maj Harnam Billawaria would be in reserve to the Bravo Company in Phase 1 and would move ahead to mop up and exploit after the initial phase had succeeded.
- The Delta Company under Sub Milkhi Singh would be in reserve for the Alpha Company in Phase 1 and would move ahead to consolidate after the initial phase succeeded.
- A troop of PT-76 amphibious tanks from the 45th Cavalry would cross the Bhairab River and go on the other bank before the attack to provide covering fire.
- All fighting elements were to be kept on one communication net for better contact and close control.
- Rifle grenades were to be used extensively, as no artillery support was possible.

- Enemy HMGs and MMGs were to be located and indicated to the troop commander of the PT-76 tanks for elimination.
- D-DAY: 15 November 1971. H-Hour: 0530 hours.

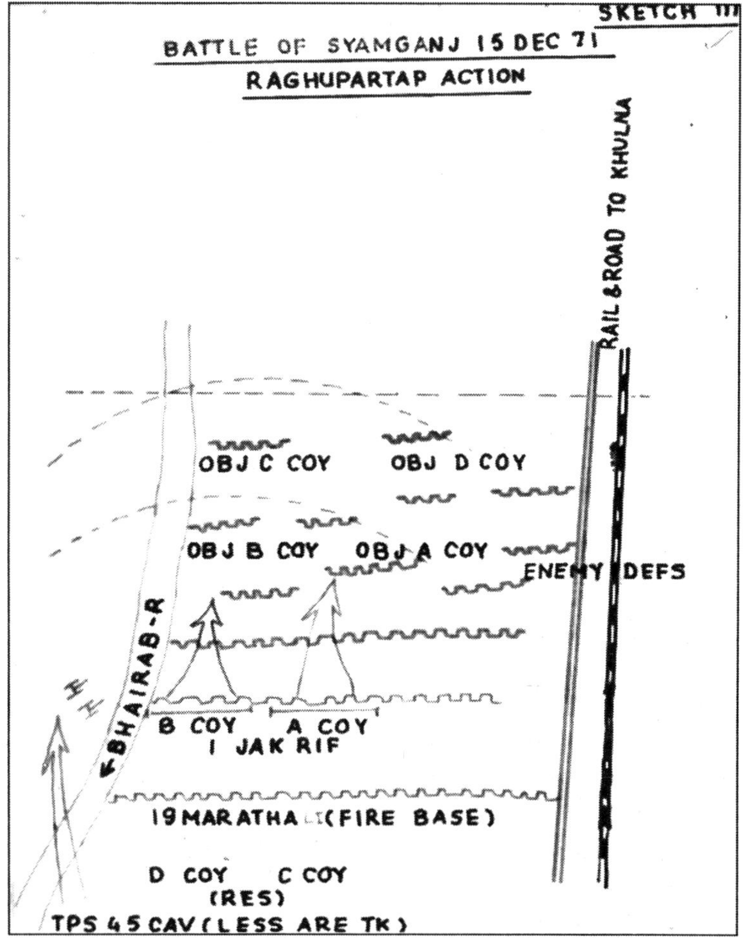

The Map of the Battle of Syamganj

Before leaving Lt Col Kapur's tent, all the officers and JCOs promised their Commanding Officer that victory would be achieved at all costs. They reminded each other about the rich history of the regiment and pledged to uphold the naam, namak and nishaan of the great battalion and regiment they belonged to.

The regimental war cry, 'Durga Mata ki jai', filled the air and the meeting was brought to a conclusion. Never before had Lt Col Kapur seen his men so charged up. The next few days would perhaps shape the way the rest of their lives would pan out. Sadly, though, a few of them would never make it back home.

Before sunrise the next morning, all the battalion troops reached the MLI firm base, trickling into small batches. Despite an acute shortage of transport vehicles, 2nd Lt Umesh had ensured that the move had been smooth. A tourist bus, which had people who had come to see Jessore from Calcutta, was commandeered to transport troops to the firm base outside Khulna.

While walking along the road head, Lt Col Kapur and his men spotted a one-ton ambulance parked in a corner. At a short distance from the ambulance, they saw a medical officer leisurely smoking a cigarette. Despite so many casualties over the last few days, not even one of them had reached the ambulance! 'This is absurd,' Lt Col Kapur told himself.

Walking on a foot track through the forested area, Lt Col Kapur was shocked to see the bodies of the soldiers from 19th MLI strewn in large numbers beside the track. Some had bullets through their heads, while others had their intestines popped out gorily. It was unfortunate to see that a handful of them had bled to death from leg and hand injuries. All of them had died because they could not get medical aid in time.

As there was no suitable vehicle track running through the forest, all these gallant men had to be carried physically by their battle-weary comrades to the one-ton ambulance, which was more than a kilometre away from the battle site. Crucial time was lost, and many of the injured men died before the doctor could even see them. Lt Col Kapur now understood why the medical officer was leisurely smoking a cigarette; casualties had hardly reached him!

'Sir, my battalion will not go in for an attack before the Army engineers construct a vehicle track through the forested area,' radioed Lt Col Kapur.

'It is tough to make one at such a short notice,' Brig Sandhu responded.

'It has to be done, sir. We are losing men without them even getting treatment. A vehicle track through the woods will help in swift casualty evacuation,' Lt Col Kapur stressed.

Without further pondering, the Brigadier assured, 'It will be done, Surinder.'

To be doubly sure, the RMO attached to 1st JAK Rifles rang the ADMO (Assistant Divisional Medical Officer) and said in no uncertain terms that lives were being lost because of bad planning by the AMC (Army Medical Corps). This expedited the track construction and the skilful and enterprising Army engineers got to work immediately.

The Army engineers had played a very crucial combat support role in the operations. The war was beginning to be dubbed as the 'Sappers War' in recognition of the contributions made by the engineers. Making foot tracks and road tracks over difficult terrains, repairing and building bridges for the faster movement of troops and clearing minefields at great personal risk were some of the tasks carried out by the sappers. All this had been done in double quick time and under the pressure of immense firing and shelling from the enemy side.

After the seamless replacement of the 19th MLI troops by his own troops, Lt Col Kapur met Lt Col Shamsher Singh again in the clearing. With him, as usual, was 2nd Lt Umesh Gupta. All through the night, this young officer had guided the battalion forward from Jessore to the attack site. He then guided each company to its location and introduced them to the Maratha guides. Even though this took a heavy toll on his body, his endearing smile stayed intact.

The trio stood there for some time, taking stock of the situation and overlooking the deployment of the troops. Suddenly, there was a long crackle sound, which pierced the eerie silence. A hidden enemy MMG had opened up. The officers immediately crouched low to take cover against the MMG.

Holding his ear tightly, Lt Col Shamsher said in a shaky voice, 'Surinder, I have been hit.'

Turning to his left, Lt Col Kapur saw blood dripping from Lt Col Shamsher's ear lobe. To prevent further blood loss, Lt Col pressed it hard and said, 'You are lucky. One inch to the left and you were gone.'

Naik Ramesh, the signalman, who was standing right behind Lt Col Kapur, tugged at his trousers, and said, '*Sahab,* IO *sahab ko goli lagi hai.*' (Sir, the IO has been hit by a bullet).

Lt Col Kapur turned right, and to his horror, he found 2nd Lt Umesh Gupta lying face down on the ground with the helmet covering his face. Hoping against hope for him to survive, Lt Col Kapur turned him around and removed the helmet, but what he saw next shook him completely.

The broad forehead of the officer had a large red hole in the middle. The MMG bullet had gone right through his temple, taking a piece of his brain, and exiting through the base of his skull at the back. In his endeavour to cover his CO from all dangers, the dashing young officer who had earlier survived many close shaves, took a fatal bullet. It was a huge setback to the battalion to lose such a bright young officer even before the battle could begin.

Adding to the unimaginable tragedy, Naik Ramesh, with tears in his eyes, said, '*Umesh sahib ne toh breakfast bhi nahi kiya tha. Unka khana mere pack mai hai.*' (Umesh sir did not even have his breakfast. His breakfast is in my backpack). It then dawned on Lt Col Kapur that 2nd Lt Umesh had also skipped his dinner the previous evening so that he could bring the battalion forward from Jessore.

Holding the lifeless body of the IO in his arms, Lt Col Kapur sobbed silently. This loss was personal. Over the last eight months, 2nd Lt Umesh had followed the CO like a shadow. Even in the months leading up to and during the war, he had performed well beyond of what was required of him.

The two had become very close, and Lt Col Kapur would often ask 2nd Lt Umesh about his family back home. 2nd Lt Umesh had lost his father when he was very young. His mother had single-handedly raised him and his younger siblings despite all the struggles. Just when she must have thought that the next part of her life would be better, she had lost her eldest son, who was also the sole breadwinner of the family!

Thinking about all this broke Lt Col Kapur's heart, but he gathered himself quickly. A battle had to be fought the next morning and he could not show any weakness in front of his men. 'The sacrifice of Umesh and all my other boys won't go in vain,' he muttered. He was ready for the battle.

A FLASHBACK

The death of 2nd Lt Umesh Gupta shakes up Lt Col Kapur. It feels as if he has lost his own child. While coming to his tent to relax for a few hours before the battle, Lt Col Kapur passes through the tents of his troops. Some of his men are playing cards, while others are glancing at the black and white photographs of their dear ones. Some others are reading letters from home thinking that it might be their last chance. The loss of 2nd Lt Umesh and the others now hits him harder.

Lt Col Kapur lies down to rest on the makeshift bed. Though his eyes are closed, his mind is racing back to the past. There was a time when he had been a 2nd Lt. He sighs, but his mind is lost in a haze of memories. He smiles at the memories of his four siblings in Amritsar; his naughty childhood and the love he received from his mother, Kamla Devi. The rustic countryside where he would play a game of *gilli-danda* or swim in the nearby pond, along with his friends, bring aromas and faces he hadn't thought of in a while. He chuckles at the memory of his father, Bishambar Das, an insurance officer, scolding him when he had plucked mangoes from trees in the neighbouring courtyards.

His eyes rest on the sky visible through the door of the makeshift tent. As a young boy in Amritsar, nights had meant listening to the stories of Maharana Pratap and Chhatrapati Shivaji Maharaj. Afternoons had meant reading spy comics and how he would practise salutes and pretend to be an officer.

Looking at the map hanging on his wall, his mind wanders to the partition. Lahore, the city he had ancestral roots in, had become a part of Pakistan. He and his family had been so hurt when they had heard the news. His father's transfers to different parts of India and frequent interactions with all kinds of people had helped him develop an all-round personality and gain invaluable exposure at a very young age.

The call letter to attend the Army Service Selection Board (SSB) interview in Bangalore was a turning point in life. The 7th course at the Joint Services Wing (JSW), Dehradun had begun in January 1952. Despite being average in physicals and academics, Surinder made a name for himself as a great team player; first in the Delta squadron at JSW and then as a part of the Imphal company at IMA.

Being a part of the squadron and company Hockey teams had made him realize the importance of working as a team. Boxing was another sport which drilled in him the spirit of never giving up. Firing and military tactics classes were his favourite aspects at training.

Following four years of extensive military training, two years each at the JSW and IMA, he was commissioned as a 2nd Lt in the famed 1/4 Gorkha Rifles (GR) Battalion of the Indian Army on 11 December 1955.

His first posting at Deva, in the volatile Chamb sector on the Line of Control (LOC), set the bearings for his career. Living with the other ranks in their barracks with meagre facilities helped him become a solid and empathetic leader who always prioritized the welfare of the men under his command.

Most of his practical knowledge about company and platoon weapons had been gathered from the outstanding JCOs and NCOs of 1/4 GR. He had observed them closely as they went about doing their tasks with a high level of operational standards and efficiency. He had then served with the 4/4 GR in the field area and gained further experience as a junior leader.

His performance at the Weapons Course at Mhow had been admirable, and his LMG instructor had reserved special praise for him. He had been appointed as the Military Secretary to the Governor of Assam in the early 1960s. He had also got a chance to rub shoulders with several senior decorated Generals like Lt Gen Moti Sagar and Lt Gen Harbaksh Singh. They had seen in him a very capable and competent officer who had all the markings to rise very high in his career.

On the personal front, he had met and married Aruna, a Supervising Housekeeper at Hotel Oberoi, on 23 January 1960. The lovely couple had welcomed their son in 1961 and their daughter two years later, in 1963. The family was complete and his career was on a high.

Eyes still closed, his thoughts take him back to Tanot, the place where he had been deployed during the 1965 War. He had been so close to seeing action against Pakistan in the deserts of the western sector, but the premature ceasefire had meant that his wish to fight a war had stayed unfulfilled.

Following many field postings at challenging places like Kashmir, Rajasthan and the Northeast, and excellent Annual Confidential Reports (ACRs) from his seniors, he had been cleared to take over the command of a battalion. His chance to lead a paltan had finally come when he was given the command of the 1st JAK Rifles near Bomdila in the North-East Frontier Agency (NEFA).

He is pulled back to the present by a particularly loud chirping from the tree nearby only to find his tent to be completely empty. Beads of sweat cover his broad forehead and well-formed eyebrows. There is an eerie silence engulfing the place and the moonlight peering in through the tent flap falls right on his fair face. He gulps down a mug of ice-cold water and looks at his watch. It is still three hours to go for the H-Hour; enough time for him to write a letter to his wife, Aruna.

Since the day he has been deployed at the border, he has written to her daily. Notwithstanding when the letters will reach her, he feels that it his duty towards the family to let them know he is safe.

He has another hour to reflect on his thoughts. After that, he has to assemble all his men for one final briefing. He must instil in them the spirit of revenge. Revenge for the comrades they lost at Burinda.

A few days back, they had learned that the barbaric enemy had disrespectfully displayed the bodies of Subedar Raghubir Singh and Naib Subedar Sukhdev Singh to the foreign media at Burinda. One of their boys, Lance Havaldar Kishan Singh had also gone missing during the same battle. They are sure he was captured alive by the enemy and shudder to think what they must have done to him.

Lt Col Kapur has to come up with a way to channel all the frustration and anger in his men to get a favourable outcome at Syamganj. The next few hours will be the most crucial time of his life as the 9 Infantry Division's primary aim of capturing Khulna hinges on the success of his battalion at Syamganj.

THE BATTLE OF SYAMGANJ

0700 hrs, 15 November 1971

The wait is finally over. The troops of Alpha and Bravo companies, 1st JAK Rifles, stealthily leave their FUP to attack the enemy. The three PT-76 amphibious tanks, which were earmarked to support the battalion, have finally crossed the Bhairab River after a delay of one-and-a-half hour. The dark early morning sky and swift current accountable for the delay. Their task will be to provide covering fire to the assaulting infantry troops.

As the roaring PT-76 tanks bomb and suppress the enemy, the forward platoons charge ahead to the enemy defences, zigzagging through the open field employing the standard fire and move drill. The chants of 'Durga Mata ki jai' rent the air as the advancing force surges ahead from both flanks.

Since no artillery support is available, Lt Col Kapur has come up with the innovative idea of using his rifle grenade boys in the first line of attack. The rifle grenades can effectively be launched up to a distance of one hundred and fifty metres. Numerous rifle grenades arc and start falling onto the enemy defences, creating a lot of attrition and panic.

The waiting enemy soldiers are initially shaken by the loud battle cry, the rifle grenades falling all around, and the speed of the Indian advance. However, they soon gather themselves and bring down sustained and accurate fire from their MMGs and HMGs. Seated comfortably over their guns in brick buildings and sturdy bunkers, the Pakistani troops fire without pause. It appears the trigger-happy troops want to expend all the ammunition they have!

Just minutes into the battle, Lt Col Kapur's radio set beeps. 'Tiger, the attack has been stalled. I repeat, the attack has been stalled. I have been hit.' It is the Bravo Company Commander, Maj K.K. Khajuria, on line.

Lt Col Kapur knows that stalling the attack so early will lead to disaster. 'Okay. Give the set to the operator,' he says tersely.

'Give the set to Sub Rikhi Ram.' The CO asks the operator to connect him to the Company 2-IC.

'Sir, Rikhi Ram has been killed,' the operator says, his voice trembling.

Lt Col Kapur had not expected this. Within the first five minutes of the battle, one of his assaulting Company Commanders has been injured and the Company 2-IC killed. He must act quickly or the matter could soon go out of hand. Troops, no matter how brave they are, need a good leader to lead them in battle.

Lt Col Kapur keeps the radio set and personally goes to where the Bravo Company has halted. Capt Arun and Capt Chauhan are walking right behind him. They are the adjutant and the Motor Transport Officer (MTO), respectively. It isn't their duty to follow the CO into battle.

Surprised to see them following him, Lt Col Kapur asks, 'Why are you both coming along?'

At once, they both answer, 'Sir, I am the new IO. I am replacing our brave Umesh.'

Not wanting to curb their spirits and enthusiasm, Lt Col Kapur just smiles and nods at them. These are the kind of men he is proud to lead. Maj Billawaria, the Commander of the Charlie Company, which is in reserve, is also told to bring his men forward and join the attack.

Meanwhile, the enterprising RMO, Capt A.L. Sharma, on hearing on his set that the Bravo Company has suffered many casualties, promptly orders the stretcher-bearers to go forward and evacuate the casualties. Moving under extreme fire, the stretcher-bearers evacuate all the wounded personnel and ensure they get a new lease on life.

Lt Col Kapur is impressed by the swift evacuation of the wounded soldiers. Giving first aid to the wounded as quickly as possible is of paramount importance in battle situations. It has a positive effect on the spirit and fighting potential of the whole battalion.

'Sir, what are my orders?' asks Maj Harnam Billawaria. He is raring to join the battle and prove his worth one more time. His courage and leadership at Maslia and Burinda have made him the CO's go-to man.

'Take over the attack, Harnam. Since Bravo Company has lost its Command element, all the troops from the Company are now under you,' the CO says, patting Maj Billawaria's shoulder.

He has immense faith and trust in the military talent of his young Company Commander.

Within minutes, Capt Arun and Capt Chauhan start attaching the Bravo Company troops, section by section, to the Charlie Company platoons. All the platoon commanders of the Charlie Company are informed about their additional strength and their responsibility towards the Bravo Company boys. The attack, which seemed to have stalled, picks up pace again in double strength!

Lt Col Kapur, disregarding his personal safety, quickly moves to check the progress on the right flank. His protection section and Captains Arun and Chauhan follow him like shadows. The party comes under voluminous MMG fire, but the skilful use of ground ensures safe movement.

Alpha Company's movement on the right flank is extremely slow. The Company Commander, Maj Harish Pant, having realized that the enemy bullets are hitting above waist level, has ordered his men to crouch very low and crawl forward inch by inch. As a result, the Company incurs very few casualties, but the forward movement is snail-like!

Digging deep into his tactical acumen, Lt Col Kapur tries to find ways to speed up the assault. He knows that if the attack progresses at this pace, the enemy will soon change tactics and aim its MMGs on the crawling soldiers. The result would be disastrous for his men.

Just then, Capt Arun's keen eye spots the MMG, which has been harassing the Alpha Company. The orange flashes from the MMG, in a double storied brick building, are barely visible to the others in the bright and sunny morning. Straining his eyes slightly, Lt Col Kapur looks at the indicated building and spots the MMG, which is raining death on his men. It has to be eliminated at the earliest for his men to have any chance of success.

'Maj Gulati, we have spotted an enemy MMG. Please destroy it with your tank fire,' Lt Col Kapur radios the Troop Commander of the PT-76 tanks.

An experienced 'tank-man' with great battlefield credentials, Maj A.K Gulati immediately agrees. 'Wilco. Co-ordinates needed.'

The co-ordinates are shared by Lt Col Kapur, and soon the PT-76 tanks, which are on the other bank of the Bhairab, get into action. Peeping out of his cupola to get a clear view, Maj Gulati marks the co-ordinates on the map he has and co-relates it on the ground. His black dungarees are helping him dodge the effects of the cold morning breeze blowing right at him.

His lips curve into a smile as he spots the troublesome MMG. The fervour of the battle takes over, and he asks his Sowar to move the tank twenty yards ahead and to the right of their position. The rumbling sound of the tank overpowers the sound of the breeze as it trots ahead to destroy its target.

Guiding his gunner to point the cannons in the right direction and angle, Maj Gulati asks the loader to load the ammunition. Fully satisfied that he will secure a hit on the first attempt, Maj Gulati orders, 'Shoot.'

Moments later, a cloud of crushed red brick is seen enveloping Syamganj. Maj Gulati and his crew have successfully hit their target.

The Pakistani soldiers manning the MMG are blown to bits under the tank barrage. The tank crew beams in satisfaction at a job well done.

To capitalize on the favourable outcome of the armoured attack, Lt Col Kapur orders Sub Milkhi Singh, the officiating Delta Company Commander, to move his company forward and assist the Alpha Company in the attack from the right flank. Thus, by 0720 hours, a mere twenty minutes after the battle has begun, all the companies are launched for the assault, leaving no reserves. This is an unconventional strategy not prescribed in any military manual. Having an attack reserve is always considered a must.

However, Lt Col Kapur thinks differently. He has observed that the enemy reinforcements are moving in quickly to replace their comrades who are either killed or wounded. The reinforcement and supply lines within the enemy brigade sector are streamlined. By using all his companies in the attack role and thereby accelerating the momentum of the assault, Lt Col Kapur aims to beat the speed of enemy reinforcements. It's a calculated risk the CO is ready to take.

Lt Col Kapur is ably supported by Capt Arun and Capt Chauhan during the entire battle. They actively assist him in seeking and identifying enemy MMG and HMG locations. Besides, they also assist the stretcher-bearers by indicating the location of the casualties. Whenever the attack seems to slow down, they go among the troops and motivate them to put in one last determined effort.

Across the Bhairab, Maj Gulati and his troop of tanks are having the time of their lives. Guided by their infantry brothers from 1st JAK Rifles, the tanks precisely destroy another enemy MMG position. An enemy HMG also falls prey to the accurate tank fire they are bringing down. Fondly called *The King of Battle,* the Armoured Corps is living up to its name in this war.

A clock tower, on which is seated the enemy artillery Observation Post Officer, is completely destroyed by Maj Gulati and his tanks. This has an adverse effect on the accuracy of the enemy's artillery fire and the threat on the advancing infantry columns is reduced.

One enemy MMG bunker, however, is proving to be elusive for the tanks. The bunker's strategic positioning and concealment has made it impossible for it to be targeted by the tanks. Attacking it physically is the only option left. The CO wants his best soldier to do this task.

The hero of Kangra, Lance Naik Meghraj is ordered to clear the bunker. His daredevil exploits during the Battle of Maslia have given him a legendary status in the battalion. He is considered as someone who can come out victorious from any given situation. Over the years, his pleasant and warm personality has made him a favourite of many in his company.

Lance Naik Meghraj can clearly see the enemy MMG bunker, located fifty yards in front. The rays of the morning sun are falling right in his eyes, but he does not blink. A fiery determination has engulfed him. For someone who likes music, he can only hear the sounds of intermittent enemy fire and the cries of anguish from his comrades who have been hit. As he steels himself for the final charge, he momentarily turns around and smiles endearingly at his CO.

Watching Lance Naik Meghraj and his section crawl ahead under a storm of enemy bullets, Lt Col Kapur has a lump in his throat. While he is confident that the bunker will be cleared, he fears he might not see many from the assaulting section again. A decisive moment in the battle has come.

Crawling inch by inch with his men, Lance Naik Meghraj briefly lets his mind go back to his training days at the JAK Rifles' Regimental Centre at Gwalior. He remembers his instructor giving him a lashing for not crawling properly through the barbed trenches. It had hurt him then, but now he realizes its value. He smiles to himself and continues.

Twenty metres short of the bunker, Lance Naik Meghraj signals his men to halt. 'If all of us charge together, the enemy will get more targets to shoot. I can't lose my men,' he tells himself. What he does next turns the course of the battle.

Ordering the rest of the section to take positions and give him covering fire, Lance Naik Meghraj gets up on his feet and makes a superhuman dash towards the MMG bunker. Firing his automatic carbine from the hip position, he soon reaches the narrow entrance of the brick bunker. Pulling a hand grenade from his vest pouch, he unpins it and flings it through the small window on the side of the bunker.

The deafening sound of the blast and the screams of Pakistani soldiers gladden his heart. When he reaches out for another grenade, he finds that his hands have been covered with fresh and warm blood. This is when he realizes he has been hit. Not once, or twice, but thrice. The bullets are embedded in his upper torso and are poking at his vitals.

The second grenade he throws also finds the mark and the Pakistani MMG is now totally disabled. One Pakistani soldier tries to run away, but he is bayoneted to death by the rampaging Indian warrior. The task given to him is complete, but he knows he will not survive.

Using the last ounce of his strength, Lance Naik Meghraj turns back and looks at his bewildered comrades. He has saved all of them from the jaws of death. Bleeding from his wounds, he barely has anything left in him. As he takes a step towards his mates, another enemy MMG opens up and shreds the gallant warrior. He falls hard on the soft grass. His large eyes staring into the clear blue sky.

Lance Naik Meghraj is dead! All his comrades watch in horror as his lifeless body lies next to the enemy soldier he has killed. They have never before seen such an act of raw courage and unflinching sacrifice. Lance Naik Meghraj has paid with his life to breach open the enemy defences for his battalion.

Lt Col Kapur sheds a silent tear for his bravest soldier. He has watched all this unfold right in front of his eyes. The sight of Lance Naik Meghraj charging at the bunker and then dying after clearing it is something he will never forget. His heart is filled with pride for the brave soldier, but with sorrow for his family, who will never see him again.

Because of Lance Naik Meghraj's berserk assault, the speed of the Indian advances doubles up. Under the courageous and cool leadership of Maj Billawaria, the Charlie Company and the attached Bravo Company troops race ahead on the left flank. Using their field and battle craft skills to great effect, the troops breach the outer perimeter of the Pakistani defences.

On the right flank, the Alpha Company under Maj Pant and the Delta Company under Sub Milkhi also make inroads in the Pakistani defences. Shouts of *'Durga Mata ki jai'* suppress the shouts of Allahu Akbar of the Pakistan army's 6th Punjab battalion. Systematically, one enemy position after another is cleared by the brave troops of 1st JAK Rifles.

Lt Col Kapur, despite being the CO, is leading the fight into the enemy defences. His presence and leadership hugely boosts the morale of his officers and men. He has multiple close shaves during the close-quarter fight and is extremely lucky to emerge from the battle unharmed. His chest fills with pride when he sees his unassuming and docile Dogra troops take on the boisterous Pathans and defeat them in hand-to-hand combat.

During the intense firefight at close ranges, 2nd Lt Jasbir Sarai's platoon is pinned down by a well-sited enemy MMG. With virtually no cover to move forward, 2nd Lt Jasbir does not have many options. He fires several rounds from the Rocket Launcher (RL) to destroy the MMG nest, but it has no effect on the concrete structure. Relentless LMG fire is also brought down, but it proves ineffective.

'A standing man presents a narrow target to the enemy,' 2nd Lt Jasbir's instructor had told him at the IMA. Seeing that the movement of his platoon has hit a roadblock, he stands up from his crouching position and raises the regimental war cry of 'Durga Mata ki jai'. Seeing their Platoon Commander stand up for the fight, the rest of them follow suit and charge at the enemy with the name of Goddess Durga on their lips.

The Pakistani MMG crew is unnerved by this charge and retreats in panic. Just an hour into the battle, the forward Pakistani defences have fallen after putting up a gallant stand. They had not expected the Indian charge to be so ferocious and swift. Their chances of saving Khulna now look extremely bleak.

Looking through his rifle green binoculars, Maj Gulati sees several Pakistani soldiers rushing in to reinforce the left flank. They are carrying an assortment of weapons, including many MMGs. He immediately reports this new and important development to Lt Col Kapur.

'Sir, I can see around a platoon of enemy troops carrying heavy weapons, reinforcing their left flank,' he says.

Sounding calm, Lt Col Kapur orders, 'Fire at them with the MMGs on your tank. My boys will then move in to land the decisive blow.'

Seconds after he has given his orders, Lt Col Kapur hears the sound of long crackles of MMG fire. He looks at the enemy's left flank and finds that the reinforcing column is running helter-skelter. Involuntarily, he looks across and over the Bhairab. He can roughly see the outline of three PT-76 amphibious tanks, which appear very small to him from this distance. These three beasts of war have helped his men immensely during the battle. He is filled with admiration for the Troop Commander and his prowess as a tank-man.

The RMO, Capt A.L. Sharma, is another officer who has played a defining role during the battle. He has been constantly treating injured casualties at the Regimental Aid Post (RAP), behind a large wall, since the battle has begun. The RAP is set-up just hundred metres behind the FUP by Capt Sharma and Lt Col Kapur. Having the RAP so close to the scene of action ensures that even the severely wounded soldiers get timely treatment. The loss of many 19th MLI soldiers in the previous attack, because they could not get timely treatment, has served as a lesson for them.

Capt Sharma also ensures that there are sufficient stretchers and two one-ton vehicles operating from the RAP to the Advanced Dressing Station (ADS). After he gives initial treatment, the casualties are put on stretchers and loaded into the one-ton vehicles. These vehicles then use the motorable road, made by the engineers the previous day, to get through the wooded area and reach the ADS, which is at the roadhead.

As a result of Capt. Sharma's medical skill, the quick evacuation of casualties by the stretcher-bearers and the prompt shifting of casualties to the ADS using the motorable road to move through the jungle, only one of the seventy-three injured dies.

There is no dearth of ammunition at any stage during the battle, largely due to the efficiency of Sub Maj Sadhu Singh. Whenever the Adjutant asks for additional ammunition, he is ready with his supply. Learning from the experience at Maslia, he has positioned himself very close to the RAP. With him are more than a dozen Non-

Combat (Enrolled) (NCE) soldiers who have volunteered to carry the extra ammunition.

Whenever the brave stretcher-bearers come from the scene of action carrying casualties and empty magazines, the NCE soldiers, under the supervision of Sub Maj Sadhu Singh, fill those empty magazines and give it back to the stretcher-bearers before they leave for the return journey. The stretcher-bearers on reaching the battle site hand these filled magazines to Captains Arun and Chauhan, the self-appointed IOs, for further distribution among the fighting troops. This 'chain system' works wonderfully well throughout the battle.

Despite the number of casualties they suffer, the troops of 1st JAK Rifles systematically continue to clear each building and bunker at Syamganj. Hand grenades are thrown, bayonets wielded, and rifles fired to eliminate all traces of enemy presence. They fight like men possessed. Never before has anyone been part of such a 'dance of death'. All the nervousness they had before the battle began seems to have vanished.

The brick buildings and bunkers at Syamganj are blown away beyond repair. Helmets of soldiers killed in action are seen all over the place. Walking through the enemy's defensive layout, Lt Col Kapur cannot help but think about the fickleness of time. Just hours ago, this place had seemed impregnable. Most of the Pakistani soldiers, belonging to the 6th Punjab and Frontier Force regiments, who were guarding this post, are now lying dead under bricks and over sandbags. They have died fighting at a place far away from their homes, just for the greed and arrogance of their overlords, who are watching over the developments from their air-conditioned homes at Islamabad, Lahore or Rawalpindi.

Lt Col Kapur sees a few enemy soldiers firing aimlessly in his direction before making a hasty retreat. The enemy withdrawal is confirmed by Maj Gulati. 'Sir, I can see the Pakis running away from Syamganj,' he says in elation.

'Keep the pressure up, Major. Engage them with your MMGs and chase them till Khulna,' the CO says. Victory is at his feet, but he does not want to take any chances. He wants Syamganj to be free of the enemy before he can finally relax and celebrate with his men. His boys have made him proud!

It's a chilling sight for the soldiers of 1st JAK Rifles as they watch their dead comrades being stretchered away. They had broken the same bread, trained with the same weapons, played the same games, and sung the same songs over the years. Being together in war had made their bond stronger. Watching them go, their bodies blooded by bullets and shells, is heart wrenching. Some have left behind old parents, while others will never see their young wives and children again.

While sanitizing the place, a Pakistani soldier is seen sitting on a small rock, waving a white flag gently. He is leisurely smoking a cigarette without a care for what is happening around him! It appears he had given up fighting much before the battle got over. On interrogation, it is revealed that the Pakistani soldier is a reservist who does not want to die in a war. He says that he has served his full tenure of duty and does not wish to continue in the army. His surrender is accepted.

Finally, after he is completely sure that Syamganj has been cleared, Lt Col Kapur passes on the success signal to Brig Sandhu. The old Brigadier is over the moon, and the elation in his voice cannot be missed. This victory has set the base for the capture of the enemy stronghold at Siramani. Khulna is now within striking distance!

The sinewy and battle-hardened Dogra troops sit down under the winter sun, basking in the afterglow of a job well done. They have been in continuous action for over a month, and the dominant victory at Syamganj is the icing on the cake. They have stormed and cleared the enemy's bastion in less than two hours. As they unwind over hot tea and a delicious breakfast of Poori and Sabji, they pray silently to Goddess Durga for protecting them in the battle.

Twenty-eight of the unit braves have died in the battle. Each of them has taken either a bullet in the chest or a bullet in the head. Without batting an eyelid, they have given the ultimate sacrifice for the country they loved so much. The RMO is tasked to make a list of those killed in action for submission to the Brigade Headquarters and the Regimental records.

Haversack lunch is prepared and distributed among all the troops before they can march ahead. Lt Col Kapur does not want to stop at Syamganj. He wants them to be the first battalion to enter Khulna. He does not intend to let the enemy have a safe withdrawal.

Before proceeding to Khulna, Lt Col Kapur salutes all the twenty-eight gallant souls who have given their all, for one last time.

He wipes away the tears from his eyes and orders Sub Maj Sadhu Singh to give all of them a cremation befitting heroes and their ashes collected to be given to their families.

Sixty-eight dead enemy soldiers are also buried under the instructions of Lt Col Kapur. These soldiers have also died doing their duty for the country they belonged to. It's sad to see that so many of them have been left behind by their retreating comrades. The madness of battle can unnerve even the mightiest of men.

The number of casualties on both the sides strongly indicates the ferocity of the battle. To suitably credit acts of exceptional gallantry by some of his men, Lt Col Kapur initiates and forwards citations, recommending them for gallantry awards. A posthumous PVC is recommended for the brave Lance Naik Meghraj. Four MVCs, including a posthumous one for 2nd Lt Umesh Gupta, are recommended. Besides, six VrCs and nine SMs for the battalion heroes are also recommended. The Brigade Headquarters also recommends Lt Col Kapur for a MVC as a credit to his outstanding leadership and gallantry during the battle. Earlier, his name had already been recommended for an MVC for his leadership at Maslia.

Thus, a splendid battle ends marking the beginning of the end of the Pakistani resistance in the southwestern sector of East Pakistan. The 1st JAK Rifles adds another chapter to its already glorious history. Each Officer, JCO and other rank of the Raghupratap battalion has done his job commendably. This is a battle which will be enshrined in their hearts for times to come.

GAME OVER

The capture of Syamganj broke the back of the Pakistan army in the Jessore-Khulna sector. Passing through the firm base secured by 1st JAK Rifles, the 4th Sikh established a roadblock astride the Jessore-Khulna road and behind the enemy lines, to facilitate the final assault on Siramani, another stronghold of Pakistan's 107 Infantry Brigade lying on the other side of the rail-road Jessore-Khulna.

The gallant Dogras of 13th Dogra and the Veer Madrasis of 26th Madras overcame stiff enemy opposition to capture Siramani by mid-day on 16th December. The daylight assault put in by 13th Dogra led to the annihilation of the enemy's Frontier Force unit. With the capture of Syamganj and Siramani, it was only a matter of time before Khulna would fall.

Meanwhile, immediately after the Battle of Syamganj was over, the 1st JAK Rifles started marching ahead towards Khulna. The Delta Company, led by the brave Subedar Milkhi Singh, was leading the march of the battalion. The company was brimming with pride and confidence, following its commendable performance during the battle.

Less than a kilometre ahead of Syamganj, the battalion hit a tar road which was burning under the scorching sun. Astride the tar road were large concrete buildings and huge sheds; it looked like a new industrial area.

From behind a large wall, which ran along the right side of the road, Sub Milkhi Singh saw someone waving a white flag vigorously. It was a Pakistani soldier wearing a khaki-coloured helmet peering over the wall. As he went closer, Sub Milkhi Singh heard the soldier saying, 'Let us stop this gruesome fighting. Our troops here and at Dacca will be surrendering.'

This was music to the old JCO's ears. He smiled to himself as he remembered the brash statements the high command of the Pakistan army had made before the war began. 'We will crush the Indian forces,' they had said. Now, here they were, throwing out a white flag to surrender meekly. Just thirteen days of official war had brought them down to their knees. Their game was truly over.

Lt Col Kapur was informed of this development and he immediately gave orders for the Pakistanis to surrender with all their weapons. He then moved forward to see for himself the intent of the enemy. From the rich experience he had in fighting against them, he knew they couldn't be trusted so easily.

His mind went back to the early days of the war, when they had started propaganda against him and his unit. To play physiologically with the minds of the Indian troops deployed inside East Pakistan, they had spread a rumour that Lt Col Kapur had been killed! This rumour had reached Mrs Kapur over the radio and she panicked. It took a visit to the station headquarters in Delhi and a letter by her husband to reassure her that he was very much alive and fighting!

Lt Col Kapur went close to the wall and said authoritatively, 'Come outside and reveal yourselves. Hold the weapons over your heads and surrender yourselves.'

A reply came back in English. In a plain, flat voice, one of them said, 'Sir, our higher-ups are planning to surrender tomorrow, 16 December, at Dacca. We are waiting for their confirmation, which is expected tonight. We have no weapons with us.'

Annoyed by their reluctance to reveal themselves, Lt Col Kapur insisted on them coming out with all their weapons or face dire consequences. He did not want to take any chances, especially as his battalion had achieved victory after a lot of blood and sweat.

Finally relenting, two Lieutenant Colonels, a few Majors and Captains, five JCOs and some other ranks emerged from behind the wall with their arms raised. They had no weapons with them. The embarrassment on their faces was clearly visible. They had not expected to capitulate so rapidly to the might of the Indian Army. The officers were smartly dressed in starched and well-pressed uniforms.

Surreptitiously, a section was sent behind the wall to check for weapons or other hidden enemy soldiers. The section carried out a thorough search of the vacant plot and confirmed that there were indeed no enemy soldiers or weapons in the vicinity.

One of the Lieutenant Colonels, who seemed to be the senior-most officer of the enemy party, came forward to speak to

Lt Col Kapur. He exuded arrogance and the humiliation on his face was clearly visible.

'Sir, we are willing to surrender and are waiting for final orders,' he said.

'How do we believe you?' Lt Col Kapur asked him suspiciously.

Raising his tone momentarily and then mellowing down again, he said, 'Sir, our war is over. Why will we fight after being surrounded on all sides? It belies military logic.'

Even though he was still doubtful, Lt Col Kapur agreed. 'Okay. We will wait till 0600 hours tomorrow morning, but to show sincerity, you must leave behind three officers, three JCOs and twenty-five other ranks, all unarmed, as our hostages.'

The Pakistani Lieutenant Colonel turned behind to glance at his men and again said, 'Sir, I repeat. The war is over for us. We all will surrender tomorrow.'

Lt Col Kapur agreed but added threateningly, 'The ceasefire is only till 0600 hours tomorrow morning. If you don't surrender, our entire division will advance and raze your army.'

The Pakistani Lieutenant Colonel nodded in agreement and left with his party, leaving behind a few of his men in the vacant plot as hostages of 1st JAK Rifles. By sundown, the entire battalion settled down in the factory buildings and bungalows in the area.

After the battalion had settled down, Lt Col Kapur immediately rang up Brig Sandhu. 'Sir, are the Pakistanis surrendering at Dacca tomorrow?'

Laughing heartily, the Brigadier said, 'Surinder, you are right. Maj Gen Jacob's plan of all our formations converging on Dacca has succeeded. The enemy has blinked.'

Relived and happy at the same time, Lt Col Kapur said, 'That's great news, sir. I will await further orders.'

Late in the night, when Lt Col Kapur and the Adjutant were glued to their transistor, listening to Indian radio to get news on the Pakistani surrender, a soldier urgently walked into their tent with a letter in his hand.

It was a letter from the Brigade Headquarters. Typed on it was a message for Pakistan's 107 Infantry Brigade, asking it to surrender. Lt Col Kapur's task was to take this letter to Brig Hayat Khan and ask him to surrender the next day.

Just when Capt Rajesh Chauhan was going out to check on the Pakistani soldiers held as hostages on the vacant plot, a Pakistani Captain arrived seeking to meet Lt Col Kapur. After checking that he was unarmed, his wish was granted. He smartly saluted to the CO of 1st JAK Rifles and sat on a chair put up for him.

'Sir, I have come to inform that our Brigade Commander and all the other Battalion Commanders will surrender to you tomorrow morning at the Aga Khan Palace,' he said, his voice clear.

Smiling at him, Lt Col Kapur said, 'I don't know where that Palace is, young man.'

'We will send a vehicle to guide and escort you,' said the Pakistani Captain before leaving.

Brig Sandhu was informed about this and he confirmed that Lt Gen Niazi, the Commander of all the Pakistani forces in East Pakistan, would indeed surrender to Lt Gen Jagjit Singh Aurora, the Eastern Army Commander, at Dacca in the evening.

Mid-December 1971, Dacca

The situation at Dacca had transformed. The bold crossing of the mighty *Meghna* river, by the Indian Army's 4 Corps, under the innovative and pragmatic leadership of Lt Gen Sagat Singh, had turned the tables on the Pakistani defenders at Dacca. Lt Gen Sagat, a hero of the Nathu La and Cho-La operations against China in 1967, once again proved his military talent and unparalleled tactical acumen, by loading his troops on IAF's Mi-4 helicopters to cross the *Meghna* river and drop the troops around the Dacca bowl for encirclement.

Had this not been done, the Indian Army would have taken several more weeks to cross the mighty river. With time at a premium, this innovative move by Lt Gen Sagat had increased the speed of the operations by ten times.

As a result of Operation Cactus Lily, the name given to the Meghna crossing operations by 4 Corps, Dacca had been completely surrounded by the unstoppable Indian forces. The relentless advance by the Indian Army's 33 Corps from the North and the advance of 2 Corps in the Southwest had also rendered the Dacca bowl untenable for the enemy.

On the orders of Gen Sam Manekshaw, Maj Gen Jacob, during a lull in the battle on the morning of 16 December, flew over to Dacca to meet Lt Gen Niazi. With him was a one-page document on which were typed the terms of surrender. Maj General Jacob was clear that he would not go back without a Pakistani surrender.

Despite being reluctant to sign the Instrument of Surrender, Lt Gen Niazi had no option but to do it. Even though there were twenty-seven thousand Pakistani troops in Dacca in comparison to only three-thousand Indian troops, Lt Gen Niazi knew that the matter could soon go out of hand.

The doubling up of the Indian advance and the threat posed by the Mukti Bahini to his soldiers and their families in East Pakistan made Lt Gen Niazi realize that discretion was the better part of valour. Assurance by Maj Gen Jacob that all Pakistani POWs would be treated according to the Geneva Conventions further convinced him to surrender. If he decided to fight on, his troops would be overrun by the Indian forces and decimated by the Mukti Bahini personnel, who were eager to exact revenge for the atrocities they had earlier faced.

The USA's Seventh fleet, which had entered the Bay of Bengal, was also chased away by the Russian warships and all hopes of the Pakistan army's evacuation through the sea had been quashed. The dominance of East Pakistan's ports by INS Vikrant, the pride of the Indian Navy, had also pressurized Lt Gen Niazi to seriously consider surrendering.

On realizing that Maj Gen Jacob wanted nothing but a total surrender, and with no external support available, Lt Gen Niazi decided to surrender. The racecourse at Dacca was fixed as the venue for the surrender on the evening of 16 December 1971. No elaborate arrangements were made. Just one table and two chairs were deemed enough for the historical ceremony that was to take place under full public and media glare.

The jubilant Eastern Army Commander, Lt Gen Aurora flew to Dacca to accept Pakistan's surrender. Even as he and Lt Gen Niazi signed the instrument of surrender, chants of 'Joy Bangla' (Hail Bangladesh!) rent the air. Soldiers from the Indian Army formed a human chain and protected the surrendering Pakistani soldiers from being lynched by the Mukti Bahini.

THE SURRENDER AT KHULNA

The surrender at Khulna, however, took longer. Brig Hayat declined to surrender and put a last ditch effort to salvage Khulna. Hence, even as the Pakistani forces surrendered at Dacca, the fierce battle at Siramani continued. Even though most of the town had been captured by 13th Dogra, a few pockets of resistance were still active.

Pacing up and down in his tent for further orders, Lt Col Kapur looked pensive. The delay in the surrender of Brig Hayat was a cause of worry. However, he knew it was only a matter of time. And indeed it was!

Early in the morning on 17th December, a vehicle from the Pakistan army carrying the same Captain who had come days ago halted outside the camp of 1st JAK Rifles. It brought a smile to Lt Col Kapur's face as he watched the young Captain walk up to him.

'You are a day late, Captain,' Lt Col Kapur said mockingly.

'My apologies, sir; our Brigade will finally surrender today,' the Captain said sheepishly.

Eager to get on with it, Lt Col Kapur said, 'Let's go immediately. I am eager to see your Brigade Commander.'

Politely declining to go in a Pakistani car, Lt Col Kapur, his Battery Commander, and a small party followed the Captain's car in their own Jeeps. On the way to the Aga Khan Palace, the liberated Bangladeshi people threw flowers on the Indian troops and thanked them for giving them a new identity.

As he stepped down from his jeep after a short and bumpy drive, Lt Col Kapur got the first look of the Aga Khan Palace. The main palace building was large and very impressive. It was surrounded by lush and well-trimmed gardens all around. Several Pakistani soldiers were seen loitering around the gardens and near the water fountains. They looked tired and smiled weakly at Lt Col Kapur as he passed by them.

The main hall of the palace was where Brig Hayat and the other officers had lined up. As Lt Col Kapur and his party approached, Brig Hayat called the other officers to attention and stood crisply saluting the CO of 1st JAK Rifles. '107 Infantry Brigade is ready to surrender,' he said, his voice choking.

Lt Col Kapur immediately passed back a salute and smiled at the Brigadier. Having been the ADC to senior generals and the military secretary to the Governor of Assam in his younger days, Lt Col Kapur was never fazed by senior officers. However, he took a moment to absorb the fact that Brig Hayat, the most clever and gallant amongst the Pakistani Brigade Commanders, was surrendering to him after weeks of what seemed like a game of chess. Over the course of the days, he had grown to admire the military leadership of the slim and grey-haired Brigadier grudgingly.

Then Brig Hayat and seven Lieutenant Colonels, who were probably the Pakistani Battalion Commanders, took out their belts and pulled their unloaded revolvers from the holsters. As per the protocol, they then held out the belts and revolvers in front of their chests.

On a signal by Capt Chauhan, two slim and smartly dressed soldiers from Lt Col Kapur's protection section promptly stepped forward. They took the belts off the surrendering officers and returned. Their drill was immaculate and pleased their CO. Even though he had never briefed them on this, it seemed as though they had rehearsed this earlier!

'I will now take you to the Headquarters of 9 Infantry Division. You can formally surrender to our GOC, Maj Gen Dalbir Singh,' said Lt Col Kapur, addressing Brig Hayat.

Brig Hayat and his officers nodded, and followed the party from 1st JAK Rifles out of the Palace. On coming outside the hall, Brig Hayat pointed at his staff car, suggesting that he would come to the Division Headquarters in it. Lt Col Kapur brushed it aside and told Brig Hayat to accompany him in his Jeep. Instructions were also given for the other Pakistani officers to follow. Brig Hayat just smiled back helplessly. The reality of surrendering was now hitting him hard.

As they reached the Divisional Headquarters, Lt Col Kapur saw a huge gathering of journalists and photographers outside. The word had spread around that Brig Hayat was finally surrendering;

a day after the main surrender at Dacca. Even as Lt Col Kapur led Brig Hayat and the others inside the building, the eager photographers clicked their pictures without pause. Flashes from the cameras were seen all around.

After introducing Brig Hayat and the seven Lieutenant Colonels to the GOC, three Infantry Brigade Commanders, and one Artillery Brigade Commander, Lt Col Kapur contacted the GSO 1 and requested him to take over the belts and weapons of the surrendered officers. He also informed him that he was going back to Khulna to settle the battalion.

As he was departing, several foreign journalists clicked Lt Col Kapur's photos and congratulated him on the victory. He nodded in acknowledgement and requested them to send him a copy of the photos, to which they immediately agreed. Unfortunately, those copies never came!

As he reached the battalion location, he immediately detailed a couple of officers to go to Khulna and select a suitable camping site for the battalion's stay in the city. He was doing what he did best. Looking after the welfare of his troops and staying away from the limelight and glare of the byte hungry media!

Brig Hayat and his troops formally surrendered to Maj Gen Dalbir Singh at the Circuit House in Khulna on the afternoon of 17th December. The GSO 1 meticulously conducted the surrender drill in the presence of the GOC, ADMS, Colonel Q, and all the Brigade Commanders.

Brig Hayat fought hard to control his tears as he moved to the table to remove his rank badges and signed the instrument of surrender, which was signed by him and the GOC using different coloured pens.

The Indian Army treated the Pakistani POWs with dignity and formed a human chain around them to protect them from the boisterous Mukti Bahini troops. One each of the pens used to sign the historic instrument of surrender was given to the Brigade Commanders, ADMS, Colonel Q, and GSO 1.

One pen was also given to 1st JAK Rifles in appreciation for the stellar role it played throughout the war. The first action of 9 Infantry Division at Maslia was fought by the battalion and the last action at Syamganj-Siramani was also spearheaded by the battalion. Finally, Pakistan's 107 Infantry Brigade had also surrendered to Raghupratap; marking the end of hostilities!

AFTERMATH

With the declaration of ceasefire on 16 December, there was joy and revelry at the separated family accommodation building at the Delhi Cantonment. Army wives whose husbands had gone to the front were celebrating and preparing for their return. They had not seen them for months and spent many a sleepless nights during the war.

Mrs Aruna Kapur was among those celebrating the victory of her husband's unit in the war. She was at a neighbour's flat enjoying some scotch. Amidst the celebrations, she suddenly sat down on a sofa, immersed in her thoughts. She had last received her husband's letter a few days back and there was no guarantee that a ceasefire meant he was safe.

'I am busy celebrating here. I don't even know whether he is safe or not?' she thought to herself.

Just then, she heard the loud yelping of her children. She ran anxiously to her flat and saw that they were sitting on their haunches in front of the black and white television. They had caught a glimpse of their father on the news channel, which was broadcasting a war report.

'We saw Papa ... we saw Papa,' they said excitedly, their eyes still glued to the television.

Mrs Kapur watched keenly, but couldn't see her husband in the crowd of soldiers. She had missed seeing him; in what was a 'blink and miss' clip. But their children had spotted him, much to her relief. He had emerged unscathed from the war, which had claimed the lives of over three thousand Indian and over nine thousand Pakistani soldiers.

The next day, on 17 December, after Brig Hayat's surrender at Khulna, Lt Col Kapur called up home to speak to his family. While the children were away, Mrs Aruna was right there; eagerly waiting for his call. Lt Col Kapur's bold and confident voice reassured her that he was totally safe. She broke down in between the call and thanked god for keeping her husband out of danger.

She had lived with the fear of losing him for over one month. Even as their children slept under warm blankets on the cold Delhi nights, she often stayed awake well past midnight, thinking about the man she loved so much. The small vacations they had gone on as a family, though few and far apart, played in her mind. She also reminisced about the day she first saw him and was swept off her feet by his rugged but handsome features.

A few days earlier, while she was busy supervising the housekeeping on the upper floors of Hotel Oberoi in Delhi, the receiver kept at the corner rang. It was her boss who had called her to report to the ground floor lobby for something urgent. The war was at its peak, and she panicked.

'What can be so urgent this late in the day?'

'I hope it's not bad news.'

Negative thoughts crossed her mind even as she waited impatiently for the elevator to reach the ground floor. In her worry and panic, she almost skipped a step as she reached the table where her boss was sitting. It was a work related call, he told her. 'I am worrying unnecessarily,' she thought.

Meanwhile, on 20 December, Lt Col Kapur had an unexpected visitor. A very well dressed Pakistani Lieutenant Colonel was brought to his tent. The officer looked clueless as he avoided making eye contact with the Indian troops.

'What brings you here, officer?' asked Lt Col Kapur, half in wonder.

'Sir, I was on leave. My unit was at Khulna and I did not know that we had surrendered,' he said, words rushing out of his mouth.

'So.?' Lt Col Kapur asked, looking bemused.

'The locals told me to surrender to you,' he said, his voice soft.

Lt Col Kapur just smiled and accepted his surrender. This was an unexpected catch well after the war was over. He felt slightly bad for the Pakistani officer who had to become a POW without actually being a part of the war!

The next few days were spent in interacting with the Pakistani POWs. While their soldiers and JCOs were over enthusiastic about talking to their Indian counterparts, their officers preferred to stay aloof.

One day, the JCOs of 6 Punjab, the Pakistani battalion which faced 1st JAK Rifles first at Maslia and then at Syamganj, met Lt Col Kapur as he was on his rounds. They spoke to him in Punjabi and praised the bravery of his battalion. They claimed that they too were very courageous men, but their officers had let them down. If they had officers like the officers of the Indian Army, who always led from the front, they would not have lost, they boldly declared.

The JCOs of 12 Punjab, the unit that had faced 1st JAK Rifles at Burinda, commended the bravery of Sub Raghubir Singh and Naib Subedar Sukhdev Singh. They also claimed that these gallant warriors were given a burial that befitted heroes.

They also mentioned that the 1st JAK Rifles was a very fearsome battalion because, rather than killing the enemy, it focused on capturing and possibly torturing them to death. This notion was set in their minds because they heard the war cry of, 'Jai Durge' (Hail Goddes Durga) as 'Pakro Murge' (Catch the hens)! This greatly amused Lt Col Kapur, but he did not correct them. He wanted this 'fear' to stay on the minds of the enemy as long as they were in his custody!

Finally, they said that they were very proud to have faced such a brave battalion. They said that the 1st JAK Rifles had earned the respect of the entire 107 Infantry Brigade for the courage and tenacity it had displayed on the battlefield. They claimed that it was no shame for their brigade and battalion commanders to have surrendered to such a brave unit.

The praise showered by the enemy was heartening to hear, but Lt Col Kapur suspected that they were trying to be friendly as they were now in his custody and were unsure about the treatment that would be meted out to them by the battalion!

Shortly after, all the Indian Army units systematically moved out of Bangladesh. All traces of East Pakistan had been wiped off. 1st JAK Rifles received orders to move to the sports stadium at Barrackpore in West Bengal and camp there. The headquarters of 350 Infantry Brigade, with two of its battalions, was moved to its permanent location at Ramgarh Cantonment in Bihar. Their task was to manage the Pakistani POWs encamped at Ramgarh.

While moving back, the battalion passed through Jessore, the town which was a terrifying battlefield just weeks ago. A Mukti Bahini JCO who had operated under the guidance of 1st JAK Rifles was waiting for Lt Col Kapur in his Jeep. He had come to receive the CO on behalf of a Mukti Bahini Commander.

After ordering the battalion to proceed to Barrackpore, Lt Col Kapur was guided to a huge building inside Jessore town by the JCO. Inside the building, Lt Col Kapur was led to huge and well-furnished office. Sitting on a chair was Capt Najmul Huda, the Mukti Bahini officer, who operated under 1st JAK Rifles.

On seeing Lt Col Kapur, he immediately stood up and saluted. 'I am so glad you came, sir. This is my new office. I am the new commissioner of Jessore,' he said, beaming proudly.

'Wow! That's great. Many congratulations, young man. I am so happy for you,' said Lt Col Kapur. It was heartening for him to see someone who had operated under him rise so high. Sadly, a few years later, he would be killed in a coup d'état. A promising life was tragically cut short.

At Barrackpore, after finding that the command hospital was nearby, the RMO, Capt Sharma went there to meet the injured casualties of 1st JAK Rifles. All of them had been first treated by him on the battlefield and owed their lives to his timely treatment. Even though some of them could hardly move, they smiled and managed to give a half salute.

The next day, Lt Col Kapur, the Sub Maj and a few officers accompanied Capt Sharma to meet the casualties. On seeing their beloved CO, the injured boys of 1st JAK Rifles broke into a loud cheer. High in spirits, they raised the regimental war cry of 'Durga Mata ki jai' and lifted their arms in unison.

Lt Col Kapur was pleased to see that his boys were recovering well. They were receiving good treatment and care. The staff at the hospital was very efficient and friendly and catered to every need of the patients. On returning to the unit, Lt Col Kapur instructed all the officers and JCOs to visit the injured troops to boost their morale.

A month later, the Army Headquarters decided to shift 2 Corps to the western sector. As a result, the whole of 9 Infantry Division, which was a part of 2 Corps, was also moved to the western sector. The 1st JAK Rifles was posted at Giddarbaha, a town close to Bhatinda in Punjab.

In mid-January 1972, Mrs Aruna Kapur joined her husband to attend the investiture ceremony at the Rashtrapati Bhavan. She looked on and cheered proudly as the President of India, Shri V.V. Giri, pinned the Maha Vir Chakra on the chest of her brave husband for his leadership at Maslia and presented him with a scroll of his gallantry award citation. All those days and months of anxiety precipitated in the form of happy tears flowing down her cheeks.

Unfortunately, despite sending twenty citations for gallantry awards endorsed by GOC 9 Infantry Division, not a single gallantry award was given to 1st JAK Rifles for the Battle of Syamganj! Lt Col Kapur's recommendation for a bar to the MVC by the Brigade Commander also vanished in thin air. This was truly perplexing, as the troops of 1st JAK Rifles had beaten back an enemy brigade at Syamganj against all odds. Therefore, the battalion had to be content with the gallantry awards it had received for the Battle of Maslia.

In late 1972, on completion of his tenure, Lt Col Kapur relinquished the command of 1st JAK Rifles, the battalion he loved so dearly. All the officers, JCOs and other ranks of the battalion bade him a tearful farewell. A CO is always close to the hearts of the men he commands, and more so, when he has led them successfully in a war. Hence, the departure of Lt Col Kapur left a lump in their throats.

Lt Col Kapur, a man who hardly showed emotions, also sobbed silently as he bid the battalion a farewell. He knew that every man of this brave battalion had played his part to ensure that his tenure as the CO was smooth. He was proud to have led such loyal and courageous troops in war, something which he would cherish all his life.

EPILOGUE

After a few other important postings, including a foreign tenure, Lt Col Kapur decided to retire prematurely from the Army in 1978, despite having bright future prospects. Being away from his wife and young children for long periods had taken a toll on him. He decided that the next half of his life would be dedicated to his old parents and family.

He was satisfied by the way his military career had shaped, and decided to settle down in Bombay to pursue his business goals. In 1979, unexpectedly, the Colonel of the JAK Rifles regiment (COR), Lt Gen G.S. Rawat, called up Lt Col Kapur and informed him that 1st JAK Rifles was given neither a battle honour nor the theatre honour 'Bangladesh'.

'A battle honours review committee has been set up under the former Western Army Commander, Lt Gen K.P. Candeth. You must come to Delhi and present your battalion's case,' the COR said.

Lt Col Kapur, who was already sour because none of his battalion braves had received a gallantry award for the Battle of Syamganj, despite him sending so many citations that were endorsed by the GOC 9 Infantry Division, decided to head to Delhi immediately. He was appalled to know that the battalion, which was acclaimed as the best in 9 Infantry Division, was being ignored when it came to gallantry awards and battle honours.

At Delhi, he met Lt Gen Rawat and his gallant Company Commander, Maj Harnam Billawaria. Over a drink at the mess, Lt Col Kapur and Maj Harnam reminisced about the 'good old' days. They spoke at length and expressed their displeasure over the battalion being ignored for a highly deserving battle honour.

The next morning, Lt Col Kapur gave a detailed account of the actions his battalion fought at Maslia, Burinda, Jessore and Syamganj to the Battle Honours Review Committee. He ended the account by stating that the Pakistani Brigade Commander and a clutch of Lieutenant Colonels had surrendered to him at the end of the war.

Lt Gen K.P. Candeth was a very considerate and pragmatic officer. He was a decorated officer with vast battle experience. His role as the Western Army Commander during the 1971 War was highly commended by all. After hearing out Lt Col Kapur patiently, he asked him to come to his office after lunch.

'Colonel, your claim that you advanced to Jessore in an autorickshaw and a fire engine is very amusing and hard to believe,' exclaimed the tall General.

'It is indeed amusing and unbelievable, sir. It looks like a scene straight out of a movie, but this happened. Trust me,' Lt Col Kapur chuckled.

With a smile on his face, Lt Gen Candeth nodded and kept the file on the table. He told Lt Col Kapur that he was satisfied with whatever he had heard and assured him that 1st JAK Rifles would get what it rightly deserved.

Soon, it was announced that 1st JAK Rifles had been approved for the Battle Honour of 'Syamganj' and the theatre honour of 'East Pakistan' for its role in the 1971 War. Even though happy, Lt Col Kapur was not satisfied. He still could not get himself to believe that no one from his battalion got a gallantry award for the Battle of Syamganj. This was something that would prick him until his last breath!

HEROES KILLED IN ACTION

1. 2nd Lt Umesh Gupta, MiD
2. Subedar Rikhi Ram
3. Subedar Raghubir Singh
4. Naib Subedar Charanjit Singh
5. Naib Subedar Sukhdev Singh, SM
6. L. Hav. Krishan Lal
7. Naik Prem Singh
8. Naik Amar Singh
9. Naik Qubla Singh
10. Naik Inderjit, SM
11. Lance Naik Ram Singh
12. Lance Naik Des Raj
13. Lance Naik Puran
14. Lance Naik Basi Ram
15. Lance Naik Chatro Ram
16. Lance Naik Rai Chand
17. Lance Naik Mahant Ram
18. Lance Naik Baldev Singh, SM
19. Lance Naik Nand Lal
20. Lance Naik Kartar Singh
21. Lance Naik Karan Singh
22. Lance Naik Sant Ram
23. Lance Naik Magar Singh, Vrc
24. Lance Naik Megh Raj, Vrc
25. Rifleman Gauri
26. Rifleman Ram Dass
27. Rifleman Uttam Singh
28. Rifleman Banto
29. Rifleman Milap Singh
30. Rifleman Hans Raj

31. Rifleman Pritam Chand
32. Rifleman Umed Singh
33. Rifleman Roop Chand
34. Rifleman Narottam Ram
35. Rifleman Balo Ram
36. Rifleman Bali Ram
37. Rifleman Sukhdev Singh
38. Rifleman Mohan Lal
39. Rifleman Amar Chand
40. Rifleman Krishan Lal
41. Rifleman Jai Singh
42. Rifleman Dharam Chand
43. Rifleman Sabho Ram
44. Rifleman Munshi Ram
45. Rifleman Baldev Singh
46. Rifleman Fauja Singh
47. Rifleman Tilak Singh
48. Rifleman Kali Dass
49. Rifleman Sunder Lal
50. Rifleman Hans Raj
51. Rifleman Sarwan Kumar

GALLANTRY AWARDS

Maha Vir Chakra

- Lt Col Surinder Kapur, IC-7684 – Maslia

Vir Chakra

- Naik Rajinder Singh – Maslia
- Lance Naik Megh Raj (Posthumous) – Maslia
- Lance Naik Magar Singh (Posthumous) – Maslia

Sena Medal

- Captain A.L. Sharma (MR-2612) – Syamganj
- Naib Subedar Sukhdev Singh (Posthumous) – Maslia
- Naik Inderjit Singh (Posthumous) – Maslia
- Lance Naik Baldev Singh (Posthumous) – Maslia

Mention-in-Dispatch

- 2nd Lt Umesh Gupta, IC-23670 (Posthumous) – Maslia

Unit Awards

- Battle Honour – Syamganj
- Theatre Honour – East Pakistan

A FEW HEROES OF 1ST JAK RIF

Lt Col Surinder Kapur

Captain A L Sharma

2nd Lt
Umesh Gupta, MiD

Naib Subedar
Sukhdev Singh, SM

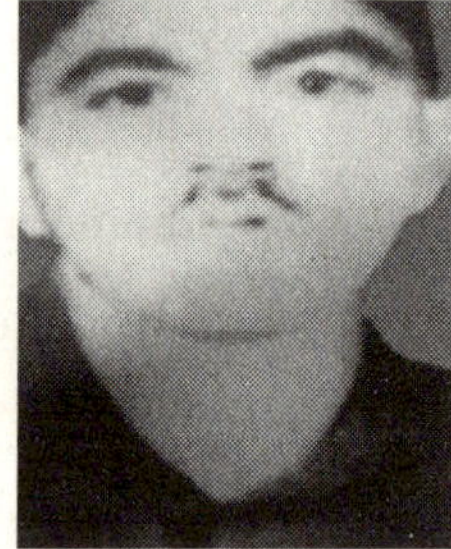

Naik Inderjit, SM

Naik Rajinder Singh

Lance Naik
Baldev Singh, SM

Lance Naik
Maghar Singh, Vrc

Lance Naik
Megh Raj, Vrc

THROUGH THE SANDS OF TIME

Lt Col Surinder Kapur taking over as the CO of 1st JAK Rifles

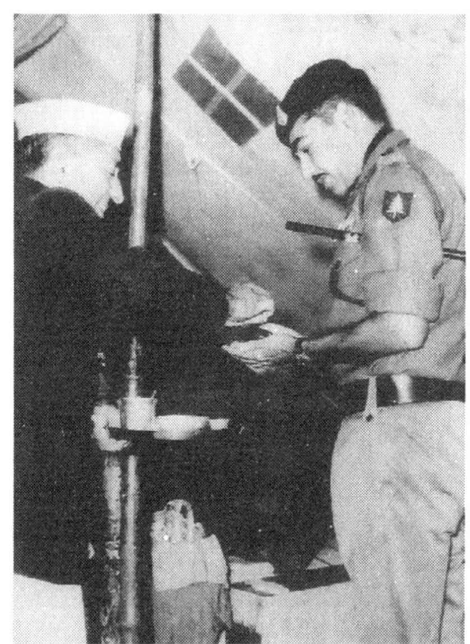

Lt Col Surinder receiving *prasad* in the unit Mandir tent.

The then President of India, Shri V V Giri, pinning the Maha Vir Chakra on Lt Col Kapur's chest during the ceremony at Rashtrapati Bhavan in January 1972

ANNEXURE 1
LIST OF ACRONYMS

- 2-IC: Second in Command
- ASC: Army Service Corps
- CO: Commanding Officer
- FOO: Forward Observation Officer
- GOC: General Officer Commanding
- GR: Gorkha Rifles
- GSO: General Service Officer
- IAF: Indian Air Force
- IB: International Border
- IO: Intelligence Officer
- JAK Rifles: Jammu and Kashmir Rifles
- JCO: Junior Commissioned Officer
- LMG: Light Machine Gun
- MLI: Maratha Light Infantry
- MMG: Medium Machine Gun
- MTO: Motor Transport Officer
- NCO: Non-Commissioned Officer
- PAF: Pakistan Air Force
- RCL Det: (of a gun) Recoilless Detachment
- RL: Rocket Launcher
- RMO: Regimental Medical Officer
- RP: Regimental Police
- 'R' Group: Reconnaissance Group

ANNEXURE 2
MILITARY TERMINOLOGY

Large Military units

- Battalion: Is an infantry unit which consists of close to nine hundred men. It is divided into four companies – Alpha, Bravo, Charlie and Delta. It also has support elements like mortar platoon, commando platoon, signals platoon, transport platoon, etc.
- Brigade: Three to four battalions form a Brigade.
- Division: Three to four brigades comprise a Division.
- Corps: Two or more divisions comprise a Corps.
- Command: Two plus Corps constitute a command.
- Army: Many commands put together comprise the entire army. It includes infantry, artillery, cavalry, services, signals, etc.

Small Military Units

- Quick Reaction Team (QRTs): A squad of six men who specialize in special and contingent operations.

- Section: Comprises eleven men led by a soldier with the rank of a Lance Naik or Havaldar.
- Platoon: Three sections make up a platoon and it is generally commanded by a Subedar, Lieutenant or a Captain.
- Company: Comprises 121 soldiers and consists of three platoons and other support elements. It is generally commanded by an officer with the rank of Major or Captain, and in rare cases by lieutenants.

ANNEXURE 3
OFFICER RANK STRUCTURE IN THE INDIAN ARMY

- Second Lieutenant: An erstwhile rank in the Indian Army, junior to a lieutenant.
- Lieutenant: Junior most rank for an officer in the army. An officer remains a lieutenant for a period of two years after commissioning. Generally, leads a platoon.
- Captain: An officer is promoted to the rank of Captain after two years of service. Generally, commands a company.
- Major: An officer is promoted to the rank of a Major after six years of service. He is generally given the command of a company.
- Lieutenant Colonel: An officer is made a Lieutenant Colonel after thirteen years of service. He is generally the battalion 2nd In Command or the Commanding Officer.

- Colonel: An officer becomes a Colonel only after passing certain staff examinations. Can command a battalion or be on the staff.
- Brigadier: A brigadier commands a brigade of troops and promotion is merit based.
- Major General: A Major General commands a division of troops and is promoted on merit.
- Lieutenant General: An officer with the rank of Lieutenant General commands a corps. Important army commands are also commanded by Lt Gens.
- General: He is the chief of the army and commands all the units of the entire army.

ANNEXURE 4
WARTIME GALLANTRY AWARDS

1. Param Vir Chakra (PVC): Highest wartime gallantry award of India. Has been given only to twenty-one soldiers to date. Getting the PVC is rare, and it is given for extraordinary acts of bravery. Its peace time equivalent is called the Ashok Chakra.

2. Maha Vir Chakra (MVC): Second highest wartime gallantry award of India. Just around two hundred odd soldiers have won the MVC. It is given for bravery and leadership of very high order. Its peace time equivalent is called the Kirti Chakra.

3. Vir Chakra (VrC): Third highest wartime gallantry award in India. Just 1200+ soldiers have received this prestigious award. Its peace time equivalent is called the Shaurya Chakra.

4. Sena Medal (S.M): It's a medal given to soldiers for performing deeds of gallantry in the face of enemy fire. Given both during wars as well as peace time, it comes after the Vir Chakra in the order of precedence.

ACKNOWLEDGEMENTS

No book, especially something which pertains to military history, can be written without the help, support and advice of certain special individuals. In my endeavour to thank all those who have helped me, if I have unknowingly missed anyone, kindly excuse me.

Firstly, this book would not have been possible without the permission and support of Lt Col Surinder Kapur, MVC. From the day I first floated the idea of a book to him, he was very sanguine and believed in the efforts which were being put in. Whenever I wanted to confirm the exact dates and locations of certain events, he was just a call away. The written matter he sent, recalling his days at war, was of immense help. Also, I can never thank him enough for agreeing to collaborate on this book. This book is for him and his boys from 1st JAK Rifles.

Mrs Aruna Kapur was gracious enough to speak to me over the phone on a couple of occasions. She recalled with a sense of pride and nostalgia the days she spent looking after her young children while her brave husband was away at war. It really gave me a sense of how a 'fauji' wife deals with such a situation, with grit and élan.

Next, I would like to extend my thanks to the current CO of 1st JAK Rifles and his resourceful officers. They helped me with the list of gallantry award winners and also sent me the names of the fifty-one heroes the battalion lost in 1971. A few maps, sketches and photographs added in the book are also courtesy 1st JAK Rifles.

Besides, a few other officers of the JAK Rifles regiment, who cannot be named as they are still in service, proved to be extremely helpful and motivating. They provided me with certain contacts which I thought I would never get!

Lt Gen Y.K. Joshi, PVSM, UYSM, AVSM, VrC, SM (Retd), a Kargil War hero and the former Colonel of the JAK Rifles and Ladakh Scouts regiment, has always been there for me like a rock. I heartily thank him for his words of encouragement and advice.

Col. Jasbir Sarai, a young subaltern during the 1971 War, gamely shared with me his memories from the war. Despite his crammed schedule, he made it a point to give me his wonderful insights.

Mr. Vikas Manhas, the soldier's soldier, has always been there, giving me his unconditional support, and so has the team Kargil Story led by Juli Sharma and Nikhil Matalia. Jai Samota, whom I consider my younger brother, was always there for help. These esteemed people are the invisible pillars of strength.

My family has been and will always be my greatest source of inspiration and strength. My grandparents, no matter what, have always backed me and my passion for writing. I am indeed lucky to have them around! My parents are the best I could ever ask for. While my father keeps telling me to push the limits, my mother patiently goes through the drafts, giving her suggestions.

My younger sister Diksha, even though busy with her professional assignments, makes it a point to always hear me out. Tanu, my wife, has been by my side whenever writing has overtaken my other priorities. She has been unconditional about her love and support. My little daughters Aaradhya and Aarya, though too young to understand what their dad does, are my source of comfort and joy. Their smiles light up even the toughest of days.

Mr. Arup Bose, my fabulous publisher, has been a soundboard. It is always refreshing to listen to him and discuss new ideas. It helps immensely that he too is a patron of military history. Mrs. Stuti Gupta, my wonderful editor, does her job seamlessly. Her prompt suggestions are always helpful. Mrs. Alisha Verma Chopra and the entire team at Srishti Publishers must be thanked for this book and how it has shaped up.

Lastly, but most importantly, I thank those innumerable heroes who fought for us and protected our sovereignty. If not for them, such books were impossible to write. It is their blood and sweat, which shines through in this book.